GREAT PIERS OF CALIFORNIA

Santa Barbara's Stearns Wharf—you walk in or ride on.

GREAT PIERS
of
CALIFORNIA

A GUIDED TOUR

JEAN FEMLING

Photographs by Marcel Mathevet

558752

CAPRA PRESS
1984

To Mama, with love

Cover and all photographs by Marcel Mathevet, unless otherwise noted.
Design by Jim Cook, Cook / Sundstrom Associates

LIBRARY OF CONGRESS CATALOGING IN PUBLICATION DATA
Femling, Jean.
Great piers of California.
1. California—Description and travel—1981-
Guide-books.   2. Piers—California—Guide-books.
I.Title.
F859.3.F44 1984   917.94′0453   84-7662
ISBN 0-88496-222-9 (pbk.)

Published by
CAPRA PRESS
Post Office Box 2068, Santa Barbara, California 93120

Contents

Bathers beside Capitola Pier, 1903. Swimmers behind them are hanging onto a rope anchored farther out, a common practice.

Introduction

"Ocian in view. O, the joy!"
—William Clark
Journals of Lewis & Clark

Out on the pier Sunday morning, grey inland and down the coast, but over the water the overcast is beginning to break up: rays of sunlight pierce the clouds, and a cluster of sailboats dances in a sudden patch of spangled water. Sixty or so fishermen are already settled in, baiting, casting, reeling, waiting....Out on the end someone brings in a bonita, and it beats frantically on the cement for a moment.

Under our feet the pier trembles faintly as ground swells grumble through the pilings and rise shoreward, crashing in their endless rhythm. Neither land nor sea, afloat nor ashore, any pier is a magical jumping-off spot, where the limitless ocean begins. This is the very edge: land's end.

Each of California's forty-three coastal piers has its own unique personality, a compound of setting, structure, geography, the circumstances which produced it, and the activities of the people who give it life.

WHERE PIERS ARE BUILT, AND WHY

Piers are constructed where the incline of the ocean floor is fairly shallow, and over sandy bottoms so that the piles, whether wood or concrete, can be driven in deep enough for secure support. And where people will be able to use them readily: hence almost all are part of a seaside community. Only Gaviota and San Simeon, serving vacationing fishermen, are far from town.

As you'd expect, Southern California, with its broad coastal plains, sandy beaches and huge urban population, also has the majority of the state's piers. California's rocky north coast has few natural harbors and only one pier in the open ocean, delightful Trinidad; though there are several others protected by bays and breakwaters.

The traditional pier was (and most often still is) a platform built on wood pilings, cross-braced; its deck often blacktopped. Sometimes pilings and deck were then sheathed with concrete. New piers may be built the same way, or may be constructed of concrete and steel. During the storms of January-March, 1983, which severely damaged many California piers and destroyed Point Arena, San Clemente, Avila and Seal Beach piers, all of the state's five new concrete and steel piers, from Ocean Beach in San Diego to Pacifica, south of San Francisco, were almost unharmed—as was old Huntington, also of concrete except for its outer end, which was damaged.

WHAT YOU'LL SEE

The view from the end of the pier is a panorama of the town and its surrounding terrain, from the magnificent reach of the Santa Ynez range behind Santa Barbara to Huntington Beach's pumping oil wells. You can see the whole sweep of the coastline, water traffic, seabirds, sometimes seals or the spout of a migrating grey whale; and sample all the coastal weathers.

WHAT'S GOING ON?

To begin with, fishing: it's free on any public California pier, and you don't need a fishing license, though you do have to observe Fish and Game regulations on protected species, size limits and seasons. Most piers have bait and tackle stands, where you can often rent fishing poles, or buy a hand line. Tackle stand operators can tell you what's being caught and which bait is most effective at the moment.

Live bait isn't available if the weather has been too rough for the bait boats to go out after it. Fishermen also use mussels from the pier pilings, fish they've snagged, or squid or shrimp from a nearby market.

You can expect to find good swimming beaches alongside most piers, and surfing in the vicinity, for which the pier is a ringside seat. And places to rent surfboards, beach chairs, skin-diving gear. At several you can buy fresh fish, live lobsters and shellfish. Many have bicycle and rollerskating concessions close by, fish and chips, postcards, saltwater taffy, and the ever-present video arcades.

A few, like Redondo and Santa Cruz, preserve the old amusement pier tradition—Santa Cruz's rollercoaster is a relic of that golden age; and on Santa Monica Pier, although it's battered and diminished, you can still ride the horses on its wonderful carousel.

HOW THEY BEGAN

In the beginning, piers were strictly business. Sailing ships tied up to California's first "pier," the wharf at Monterey, in 1845, when that city was still the capital of Alta California and part of Mexico. Whalers set up their whaling stations complete with piers from Crescent City as far south as Goleta, just above Santa Barbara.

The North Coast's rolling hills black with timber drew loggers and sawmill-builders whose main—sometimes only—connection with the outside world was the schooner which brought them supplies, passengers and mail and hauled away the lumber to build cities in the south.

California's rocky north coast bulges outward, and the farther from shore you travel, the longer the trip. Hugging the coast had its risks; rocky reefs, fatal miscalculations in a sudden blinding fog. With few natural harbors, most often the schooners had to put into a "doghole" port and tie up to a pier barely sheltered from the open sea, or load their lumber by cables slung from the cliff.

Whatever its hazards, many preferred to travel by sea: roads were few and hazardous, and the journey by stagecoach long, uncomfortable and sometimes bruising, with the added chance of highway robbery. In the 1880s the steam schooner began to supplant the windships; but, steam or sail, dozens of ships came to grief on that watery road. Historians estimate that fully half of the coastal steamers were lost.

At the height of travel by sea, steamships of the Pacific Coast line tied up to the wharves at Santa Cruz, San Simeon, Cayucos, Port Harford (now Port San Luis), Gaviota, Santa Barbara, Ventura, Hueneme, Santa Monica, Redondo and Newport—all regular stops on their routes.

As the growth of railroads and the highway system ended coastal shipping, commercial and sport fishermen were already putting the old wharves to good use. Seaside resorts and luxury hotels also built piers to provide a cooling promenade over the waves. Most were destroyed by storms after a few seasons: none survive.

Several present-day piers sprouted ahead of their communities, built by enterprising real estate developers who used the pier to lure possible customers. A simple wooden pier built out beyond the breaker line brought an astonishing variety of game fish within range, and nearly every coastal community soon had its own fishing pier.

Whenever possible, new developments lay along the routes of the Pacific Electric Railway, whose stretching tendrils allowed residents to work in Los Angeles and ride the Big Red Cars home to a green suburb or a seaside town. The developers of Huntington Beach swapped part of their land and renamed their town after Henry Huntington when he extended his trolley line to the foot of the pier.

Tourism also thrived on the interurban system, which carried visitors and residents alike to the ocean front and gave rise to the great amusement piers at Santa Monica, Ocean Park, Venice, Redondo, Long Beach and Seal Beach.

From the 1910s onward, these piers with their rollercoasters, carnival booths and dance pavilions over the surf regularly drew thousands to the seashore. Today barely a trace of them remains, their life drained away by changing transportation habits and inland theme parks like Disneyland and Magic Mountain. The piers which survive or supplant them offer quieter, water-oriented recreation.

PIER OR WHARF?

Wharf is the older term, signifying their working function; from the Old English *hwearf*, it meant first a turning place, and then a busy place on a river or seashore. *Pier*, a more inclusive term for a structure over the water with various purposes, came into general use after 1910.

What Americans call a pier is in some parts of England a jetty, from the French *jetée*, a leap—into the sea. And pleasure piers are a legacy of Victorian England, the first being built at Brighton in 1823.

WHO GOES THERE?

In smaller towns, just about everybody. Big-city piers draw a fascinating ethnic mix, and every group brings its own customs and fishing techniques to the pier; Japanese, Samoans, Filipinos, Mexicans, Vietnamese, Midwesterners accustomed to lake fishing, Louisianans from the bayous. For some, fishing is an important source of food, and they fill a couple of buckets with no-limit fish on a Saturday afternoon. Where else can you get twenty pounds of fresh meat for a couple of hours' work? And for city-dwellers generally, the pier is a breath of life, a chance to clear out the smog and fill your lungs with sea air.

WHAT THEY'RE REALLY GOOD FOR

The truth is, you're not required to *do* anything out here. In less frantic times, the local pier was the place for a leisurely promenade. A natural tranquilizer, it's still a good prescription. The salt-water cure: take one good pier, slowly....

The sun melts away the last of the morning fog, and seven pelicans cruise by single-file, gliding just above the water. Look, there's a seal playing just this side of the breakers. Somebody has a ball game on his radio, and somebody else is explaining why you're always supposed to bleed a bonita as soon as you get it. Nobody's in a hurry.... Mostly, out on the pier you understand that you're not really on the way to somewhere else. You're already there.

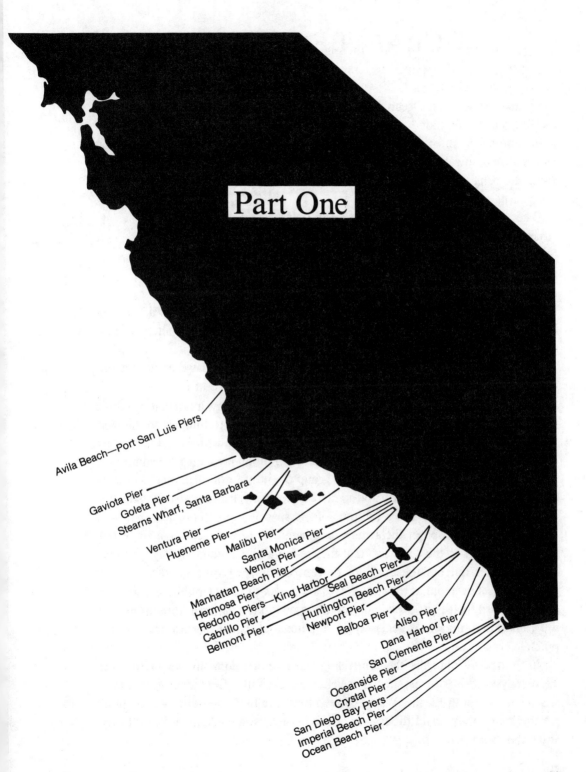

Part One

Avila Beach—Port San Luis Piers

Gaviota Pier
Goleta Pier
Stearns Wharf, Santa Barbara
Ventura Pier
Hueneme Pier
Malibu Pier
Santa Monica Pier
Venice Pier
Manhattan Beach Pier
Hermosa Pier
Redondo Piers—King Harbor
Cabrillo Pier
Belmont Pier
Seal Beach Pier
Huntington Beach Pier
Newport Pier
Balboa Pier
Aliso Pier
Dana Harbor Pier
San Clemente Pier
Oceanside Pier
Crystal Pier
San Diego Bay Piers
Imperial Beach Pier
Ocean Beach Pier

OCEAN BEACH PIER

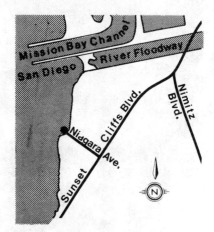

Unlike most piers, Ocean Beach looks designed, the product of a single vision. A dynamic thrust of steel and concrete angles down toward the water and then rises, shooting over the sea to end in an unequal pair of wings, bent.

The best way to take in the whole structure at once is from its head on Niagara Street, at the top of a rocky bluff which falls away beside it. On the adjacent parking lot and beach you are about thirty feet below, looking up at this entering ramp. A stairway leads up from beach level, and the landward end of the pier is supported by pairs of large hexagonal pillars, widely spaced.

"We wanted to leave the beach as open as possible, and we could get the equipment for the big piles in here," said Greer Ferver, the San Diego structural engineer who designed the pier.

At 1,971 feet, Ocean Beach is believed to be the longest concrete pier in the world. The northern arm of the finishing T is 193 feet long, and the southern arm extends 360 feet. In the original construction plan they were the same length; but when building was already underway, a group of enthusiastic San Diegans raised $92,000 more to extend the arm and so increase the pier's fishing capacity. Because of this addition, the pier has a full mile of rail space.

The gull-wing shape of the arms strengthens them by presenting a staggered pattern of pilings to the waves, so that they're not all hit simultaneously. Further, the rising pier mirrors the angle of descent of the pier bottom: the water is twenty-six feet deep out at the end. Waves are bigger in deeper water, and the pier angles upward to keep its deck and everything on it out of reach of those waves. A wave's maximum height is generally 70-75 percent of the still water depth at that point.

In Southern California the controlling wave comes from two major sources, Ferver says; nearby storms, such as the chubascos off Baja California, and distant storms in the South Pacific. Waves formed there are the more serious concern of pier-builders—they travel thousands of miles, but lose very little energy till they strike the shore.

12

"Oh, this pier has been overtopped a few times," Ferver said. "It was the first one we built. We've learned a few things from it."

Halfway out, a bait and tackle stand provides fishermen with live bait seven days a week (if the boats have been able to go out for it), and novices can buy a hand line to try their luck. Catches here include cabezon, halibut, croaker, sharks and sand bass.

Alongside it the Sea Dawg, also open seven days a week, has fish and chips, chowder and the usual fast food. It's a neat, pleasant place with windows all around, big hanging plants and a sea-dragon figurehead; the table-tops are hatch covers which have been fiberglassed.

The pier, built in 1966 and dedicated by Governor Pat Brown, is the first pier to be built at this spot, though it had been discussed by San Diegans since 1912, at least. On the downcoast side there are rocks inshore, and tidal pools. These rocks were once covered with mussels, and an early name for the spot was The Mussel

Beds: San Diegans used to come out here by buggy and wagon for a day's outing. In 1870, 200 Old Towners held their Fourth of July celebration out here, lured by an announcement promising seals on the beach, calf's head, and mussels fried, roasted and boiled, all free.

Surfing is good on the upcoast side of the pier, between here and the jetty marking the entrance to Mission Bay. If the pier is new here, surfing is not: during Ocean Beach's Hawaiian Days in 1916, Olympic swimmer Duke Kahanamoku gave a surfing exhibition.

The little community of Ocean Beach, now part of San Diego, was quiet until the '60s brought an influx of street people, attracted by the beach and relatively low rents. The result was friction between young and old and renters and owners, and bad words for absentee landlords. In one confrontation in 1968, the pier itself was cleared by the police.

Today the three-block business district on Newport is a mellow mixture of bikini boutiques, Mexican food and paperbacks, Lowndes Department Store, the Strand Theater and a big Cornet dime store, health food and a drugstore that opens at 8:00 A.M. Renters and retirees apparently agree that they want no developers or high-rise apartments. A faded bumper-strip says "Keep OB the Way it Was."

On weekends the pier is alive with fishermen and walkers and kids of all sizes. Overhead the big jets taking off from Lindbergh Field temporarily drown out conversation and the scream of the seagulls. In the Sea Dawg, someone is singing along with the radio, a soppy western number..."I'll be there before the next teardrop falls." Two pelicans are perched on top of the restrooms, and the brown one, Pete, is very good at catching anchovies people toss up to him...only sometimes one sticks sideways in his pouch, without the usual sea-water to wash it down.

The last time we were there, on a grey windy evening, we heard only the spatting of the breakers through the pilings and the muted whoosh as they broke onshore: there were no pelicans and no people, except for a few diehard fishermen. A big man in red checked shirt and cowboy hat had settled in on the bench opposite the bait shop with eight tall cans of beer. Five were already open.

IMPERIAL BEACH PIER

Imperial Beach Pier is a place you have to be looking for to find. It lies on a stretch of flat, sandy surfing beach, bracketed by the Coronado Bay Bridge and the brown hills of Mexico. Fire and storms have left the pier fishermen only a wooden stub, fifteen lampposts to the overhead sign proclaiming *Most Southwestern City in Continental U.S.*, and nine more lampposts to the end.

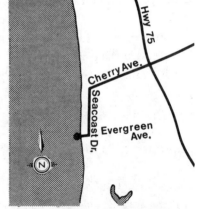

No bigtown flash or hustle here—the quiet neighborhood is little stucco houses and beach cottages, like Venice or Balboa forty years ago. On a crosspiece under the pier somebody has painted *Beautify IB—Kill a Junkie.* The sunset turns the clouds scarlet and rose darkening to purple, and a fisherman baits his hook, casts, leans and waits.

A young mother has brought out her baby in his stroller, and he points and jabbers at the lights on the moving water. Downcoast, the high ridge of Tijuana is pricked with points of light, and upcoast San Diego is a luminous haze beyond the long shallow arc of glowing amber beads marking the Coronado Bridge. "We lived in Georgia for seven years, and that was okay," she says, "but not like this. I'd rather live here than anywhere."

SAN DIEGO BAY PIERS

Inside San Diego Bay there are three public piers. Shelter Island and Embarcadero Marina Park are open twenty-four hours a day, and each has bait and tackle and an up-front view of harbor life. Farther south, peaceful National City Pier, tucked among lumberyards and docks, is a favorite fishing spot for kids in that area.

In the early 1900s, Coronado's Tent City provided a vacation at the beach for many. Hotel del Coronado (background) had two pleasure piers for its guests.

CRYSTAL PIER

Crystal Pier, under construction in Pacific Beach, was the destination of this Parlor Car Tour in 1927.

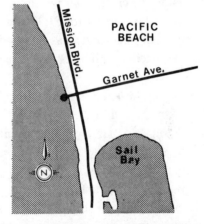

Coming down Garnet Avenue, Pacific Beach's main street, you begin to see the broad arch bridging the street and anchored by two-story buildings. Against the blue stucco the sign announces *Crystal Pier* and *Motel*: half private and half public, Crystal is the only pier on the coast where you can sleep over the ocean.

The wooden pier is closed off by a high chain-link gate, opened by key or from inside the adjoining motel office. The first 200 feet beyond are lined with blue-trimmed white cottages complete with wooden window-boxes filled with hot pink geraniums. The rest of the pier, and its tackle stand, belongs to the fishermen and the pedestrians.

That's not quite as much fishing space as there used to be, since the 1,000-foot pier lost 280 feet in the '83 storms. The weathered planking is patched with pieces of metal, and sand has been piled out on the end, evidently to add weight and minimize the rolling.

Each cottage has a living room, kitchen, bedroom and bath, and its own section of deck facing out. Shutters on the cottage windows are light blue with cutouts, a different nautical design for every cabin—lighthouses, whales, swordfish, a happy fisherman.

Mary Walsh and her husband, Bob, have been managing Crystal Pier since

1960, and several of their customers have been coming here for much longer, Mary says: one lady, an excellent fisherman, has only missed one year since 1940, and another has been coming out from Salt Lake since 1938.

"And we have doctors in town who send us their patients right from the hospital, to finish recuperating here," she declared. Residents can sit in weathered wooden chairs on their own decks and watch the surfers on either side of the pier, or drop in a fishing line. From here you can see San Diego's Point Loma stretching southward, and the bulge of La Jolla to the north.

Out here, with the pier gently rolling underfoot, it's easy enough to understand what happened to the first Crystal Pier. Built to attract land buyers, as many piers were, the pier opened in 1927 with balloon ascensions, pink lemonade and fireworks to draw the crowds. The biggest attraction was the stucco ballroom, all arches and towers, on its outermost end.

A pleasure-palace, it had cork flooring so you could dance all night without getting tired, muralled walls, and colored lights on the high balconies reflected in the glittering crystal ball which gave the pier its name. Admission was by ticket, five cents a dance; or for $1.25 you got a private loge for the whole evening, with overstuffed chairs and sofas right next to the bandstand. A ten-piece dance band in yellow tuxedos with black lapels played on opening night—and on closing night, too, as it happened.

The elegant, massive building lacked adequate cross-bracing, and swayed distressingly in all but the gentlest surf. To counteract the effect the owner, Neil Nettleship, ran piano wire through all the lights and hanging fixtures to immobilize them, to reduce the vertigo caused by surf motion and compounded by the swaying of the lights.

Worse yet: Nettleship, swimming under the three-month-old pier, noticed that the pilings looked peculiar. They were already being eaten by marine borers, because the pilings hadn't been creosoted. Both ballroom and pier had to be condemned. In payment, Nettleship offered the bandleader four lots on Garnet. He took instead the chairs and sofas from the loges to raise cash for his musicians.

The remodeled pier with the present cottages opened in 1936. Heavy surf and a 7'5" tide in 1953 damaged it and dumped one cottage into the ocean. Most of the damage was caused by battering from the wreckage of two forty-foot barges offshore which broke up and were driven onshore, shearing off several pilings.

Upstairs in the arch itself there are two apartments on either side. In the bar at street level in the upcoast side of the arch, seven or eight regulars are already engaged in a lively discussion at ten o'clock on a grey Thursday morning. The geraniums have already been watered...a pigeon alights on top of the *Please don't feed the pigeons* sign and leaves his mark. Crystal Pier lives.

OCEANSIDE PIER

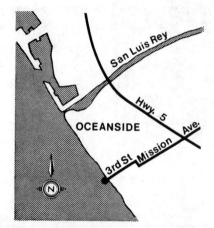

Oceanside Pier, once the queen of the south coast, lives on in reduced circumstances. From its imposing entrance, twin twelve-foot wide concrete ramps with squared balustrades of cream and tan sweep down 360 feet from Pacific Street on the bluff to join at the base of the pier itself, where a ramp and two side stairways lead down to the beach.

But beyond this point, the pier itself is an anticlimax. Partly destroyed by storms and fire, only part of the wooden pier and four outsets remain. Before the big storms of '83 closed it, the rickety pier swayed in the swells like a dinner table wanting to dance. It has since been rebuilt, repainted and re-anchored. Below it, the beach is sometimes ravaged and its rocky base exposed by the waves—the marina built upcoast has changed the ocean currents, and the sand which formerly replenished the beach doesn't always get here now. Oceanside's first pier and California's farthest-south shipping wharf was built here before 1890, when inland ranchers were already coming to the "ocean side" to escape the summer heat. Periodically damaged and restored over the years, the present entrance and adjacent stadium and band shell were built in 1926. Refurbishing in the late '40s extended it to 1900 feet plus a floating dock, and the pier was the center of activity, with boats to the fishing barge anchored three miles offshore, swimming contests, beauty pageants and Fourth of July fireworks.

Today you can get tackle and snacks nearby, but otherwise the area around the pier is languishing, waiting for the city's new development plan to revive it. Snug and trim now, the pier is much favored by fishing families—one morning it was a family of six speaking Tagalog and all catching smelt, even the littlest with a line in the water, getting instructions. Oceanside is a respectable commoner now; a survivor.

Entrance to San Clemente Pier is bridged by Amtrak train, letting beachgoers disembark. Ocean-front bluffs are covered with houses and apartments.

SAN CLEMENTE PIER

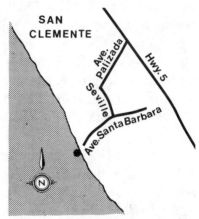

The first challenge San Clemente Pier offers is actually finding it—unlike other coastal towns, there's no direct route to the beach. Once you make your way over the hills, you'll find yourself on a sloping, land-scaped parking lot with the pier tilting out below on that huge silver platter, and up here lawns, benches and new walkways of red cement grooved like rounded blocks, curving down to—the railroad tracks.

They run straight along the ocean front at the inside edge of the beach, and four times a day the Los Angeles-San Diego Amtrak honks into view, slowing cautiously and sometimes stopping at the foot of the pier to debark or take on passengers. The central entrance to the pier is a red cement landing and twin flights of steps which lead down under the tracks.

The pier itself was one of those hard-hit by the '83 storms: its outer half with T end, tackle stand and neat, cozy cafe was torn away, and another section demolished just at the surf line. The damage has already been repaired and the pier is once again open for business—which is in fact booming, thanks to the new restaurants added on either side, just above the water's edge.

Out on the pier you're in a vast world made more spacious by contrast with the built-upon bluffs rising from the long straight beach. Black-suited surfers strad ling their boards rock gently on both sides of the pier. . .the bottom is nearly level here, and long breakers generally form a good distance from shore. Downcoast on the point you can just make out Casa Pacifica on its bluff surrounded by foliage, where the Richard Nixons lived a while back.

Saturday morning fishermen. . .among them a few older couples settled in with folding chairs and attached parasols; and several Marines from nearby Camp Pendleton, in swimming trunks and distinguishable from local youths only by their crew cuts.

For that interesting trip down here, we have Ole Hanson to thank, who gave the town its distinctive layout, and then threw in a pier. Back in 1925 during the post-World War I land boom, Hanson dreamed up San Clemente, "this Spanish village by the sea," where all the houses would be white with red tile roofs. He had 125 acres of coastal hills surveyed and laid out the lots, insisting that the streets be eighty feet wide—his engineer thought fifty or sixty would be quite sufficient.

When the Orange County Board of Supervisors refused to accept his plan, Hanson filed it as a surveyor's map, and so owned all the streets himself, paying the taxes on them till San Clemente was incorporated. Hanson predicted that the whole south coast would be "built up solid in a few years, so that one could toss an orange from housetop to housetop from San Diego to Los Angeles."

On a day in December, having advertised heavily in the Los Angeles papers, Hanson was ready. He pitched two big tents up on El Camino Real, fed lunch to a thousand or so prospects who waded in through ankle-deep mud from the previous night's rainstorm, and then told them about his new city. They bought $125,000 worth of lots by nightfall, and forty percent of the first units within forty days.

To enhance his city Hanson donated 3,000 feet of beach front to San Clemente and then gave the town this pier, built in 1928 by twenty-five men and an unrecorded number of mule teams.

Stories circulated that the pier, along with other coastal areas, was used to smuggle liquor into the country during Prohibition. "They said" that small boats brought cases of whisky in under the pier, which were pulled up through a trap door in the floor of the cafe. That cafe is long gone, lost in the big storm of '39. Its successor with the giant fish-shaped sign on top is gone, too, but a mobile bait and tackle stand in a van stations itself on the end of the pier every morning, opening for business at 7:00 A.M.

Today San Clemente Pier seems to have more traffic than before their most recent disaster. The two buildings flanking the base of the pier, formerly the domain of the local boat club, are now a seafood restaurant on the downcoast side and an oyster bar upcoast, plus an outside counter where you can get such "fast food" as a salmon sandwich or a loaf of sourdough.

Both sides have outdoor dining decks over the surf line with the breakers crashing underneath and good views in both directions, Dana Point upcoast like a giant alligator's head. As the last daylight fades the lights come on under the deck, gilding the diehard surfers, turning the water grey under the tumbling froth and illuminating a sleek black-and-white cat prowling the timbers in search of a sleeping pigeon. Olé! Olé!

DANA HARBOR PIER

Tucked inside the extreme west end of Dana Point Marina is Dana Harbor Pier, a small, wooden, shallow-water fishing pier complete with tackle-and-food stand. It's a grand place for people-watching, with grassy lawns and picnickers opposite, a sand beach and swimming, and the brilliant sails of windsurfers—you can rent these and other water gear nearby.

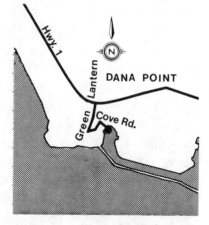

Just beyond the pier, nearer the breakwater, a marine museum has been opened. It's landscaped with native California plants.

The marina's docks and jetties offer more fishing, and there are restaurants, bars, curio shops and a fish market, plus sportfishing boats going out regularly. January-March you can take a whale cruise to watch the California grey whales migrating northward along the coast, lifting their great flukes as they sound—a deeply satisfying sight.

ALISO PIER

Aliso Pier in South Laguna, among the newest of California's piers, is also the most unusual. You follow Pacific Coast Highway over the hill, and *Zap!* there it is—an improbable structure, grey, trim and slender-legged, its diamond head like a great arrow pointing out to sea. Other piers march into the ocean level as a floor: Aliso rises from the shore, angling upward throughout its length.

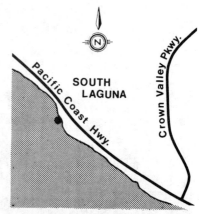

Designed by Greer Ferver, a San Diego engineer, and built in 1972, Aliso is a pleasure to look at and walk on—in fact, it was given an Outstanding Design Award by the American Institute of Interior Designers; and it's finally beginning to make its mark as a fishing pier. The diamond head, measuring 120 by 180 feet, was specifically designed to provide the maximum amount of railing space for fishermen.

The pairs of hexagonal white concrete pilings which support the pier were

precast, and then floated in and set into place by a monster machine, Spider I, which had eight legs and moved by retracting and relocating them, four at a time.

The 620-foot structure, capped by a lightweight concrete deck, was designed to be more durable and require less maintenance than traditional wooden piers. For example, the pier banister is of *apatung*, an extremely hard, dense tropical wood which resists scarring.

Aliso Beach and the pier lie at the mouth of Aliso Creek, which has been a vacation spot for nearly a hundred years. In the 1890s the Shakespearean actress Helena Modjeska camped here with friends to escape the inland heat. Laguna Beach was one of the few areas in Orange County not part of any Spanish rancho, and consequently it was available for homesteading during the 1880s and '90s. You can still see some stands of eucalyptus in the area, planted by homesteaders to satisfy government requirements.

Today the rocky bluffs and the hillsides along the highway are filled with houses, and upcoast you can see the town of Laguna Beach spreading up the hills. Little-used at first, Aliso Pier has become more popular as the south county develops. The pier was built right here because this bit of coastal land became available, itself a rare occurrence.

You can park on either side of the highway—there's an underpass from the inside lot. The pier's entering ramp wraps around a handsome concession building at the foot of the pier which houses a combination tackle and fast food stand, and some video games.

Aliso is probably better able than most coastal piers to withstand heavy storms and wave action. Its rising angle reflects the pronounced slope of the beach and the ocean bottom, which brings the breakers in quite close—some days they're real sand-busters. The beach is covered with coarse, clean sand, and beyond the little cove in both directions you can explore the rocky shoreline and the tidepools, rich in marine life. It's a pleasant spot to wander, or just relax and contemplate that pier.

BALBOA PIER

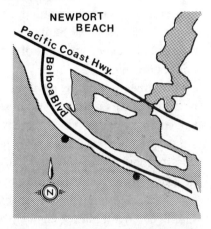

U p on the roof of Ruby's on a hazy morning, waiting to be called for breakfast...this is O-K. Since the cafe-and-tackle building was reopened in 1983, life has returned to Balboa Pier.

Ruby's is a slick little '30s modern shape, rounded corners and a red neon sign, whose classy restoration won a county architectural award. Inside, too, it's a '30s diner, all red and white with chrome counter detailing, old Coca Cola posters and red plastic booths and stools; the waiters wear black plastic bow ties and the music is all vintage swing, Artie Shaw, Benny Goodman and suchlike—a nod to the vanished Rendezvous Ballroom, which once stood a block from here.

Palm trees line the walk and shade the wide lawn at the foot of the pier with its little white bandstand, where concerts are held on summer Sunday afternoons, and between-times kids stop to adjust their skates and an occasional guitarist sits and plays to himself. Flocks of sailboats pass noiselessly, and the place mostly has a placid, small-town feeling.

Out here the surf is barely audible: the ocean bottom falls away more steeply at this end of the peninsula, and the breakers tend to be sand-busters, rearing up close to shore and shaking the ground underfoot. Just downcoast you can see the jetty which protects the mouth of Newport Harbor, which is where all these sailboats are coming from. The angle formed by jetty and beach is known as the Wedge, a conformation giving rise to impressive (sometimes immense) breakers which draw the most experienced and daring body-surfers, and people to watch them.

The wide beach from here to the jetty is fairly deserted, used only by a few joggers and kite-flyers, and on its inner margin patches of low-growing seashore vegetation spread undisturbed. The fire rings on either side of the pier are popular, especially on mild evenings.

Beyond the lawn at the foot of the pier lies a baseball field often occupied by a neighborhood game or the swooping flight of remote-controlled model planes, and there are children's climbing bars on the sand. Just across the Boardwalk at the Studio Cafe you can hear live jazz at night; and on Sunday afternoon, local musicians come in and jam, and leave the windows open.

What you don't see from here is Newport Bay, just two blocks away.

All settled, prosperous...it's hard to remember that the Balboa Peninsula, whose sandy arm shelters the thousands of boats and the island and waterfront homes in the harbor, is brand new, geologically speaking: it didn't really exist before 1825, when the Santa Ana River changed course and began building the peninsula by depositing tons of sand and silt carried here from inland mountainsides and canyons.

Both the pier and the pavilion were built in 1906 by developers eager to attract potential buyers to this nearly deserted sandspit. The lumber for them had to be hauled in by barge, since there was no wagon road into the area yet. Henry Huntington extended his trolley line on down the peninsula, after being given a fifty-six foot right-of-way and a donation of $19,000; and on July 4, 1906, in that time-honored rite, a load of excursionists arrived on the first of the Big Red Cars for a free barbeque. The Los Angeles-Balboa trip took about an hour—a time not shortened any in almost eighty years.

The first water-to-water flight was made from alongside Balboa Pier, on May 10, 1912 when Glenn Martin flew the hydroplane he'd built to Catalina Island and back, bringing the day's mail back with him. It was then the longest and fastest over-water flight ever made.

In September 1939, the tropical *chubasco* that damaged most south coast piers also took off the T and the last 100 feet of this one. During the storm a 33-foot cruiser capsized in the harbor channel, drowning a woman, and the 140-foot yacht *Paragon*, with sixteen aboard, went aground on the tip of the jetty, had its side torn away and sank in twenty feet of water.

Balboa, a popular "summer rental" spot, is jammed to a standstill on summer weekends; but the majority of its residents are year-round, with a pleasant little business community here to serve them, including the Balboa theater, which shows old U.S. and foreign movies.

Down the Boardwalk the Rendezvous Ballroom, once home to Stan Kenton and other swing-era greats, has given way to a block of anonymous condominiums; but the Balboa Inn remains at the foot of the pier. The familiar Spanish colonial pile was built in 1930, designed by Walter Hagedohn, the architect of Los Angeles' Union Station. Renovated in 1974, the Inn survives intact with its red roofs, tiled fountain and outside stairway running up alongside the oddly narrow courtyard.

Just opposite, at Oceanfront Bicycles, you can rent three-speeds, ten-speeds, tandems, tricycles or roller skates, if you'd like to explore the area on wheels. And if you hang around late enough, you can go back out to Ruby's at night and enjoy that view. Hmm...the older section of Corona del Mar has a big dark patch; no street lights there, I guess. And that gauzy, luminous cloud beyond the point and farther downcoast, resting against the hillside—are you sure that's Laguna?

NEWPORT PIER

Hiking up the curving ramp of Newport Pier—its original was designed for trains, not people, almost a hundred years ago—you find yourself on a comfortable, straightforward wooden pier a world away from Newport's glossy sporting set, belonging instead to the fishermen. They've been coming here from across town or across the county since the beginning, to stake out a yard or so of rail and see what's biting... making the place theirs again, for a few hours anyway.

Traditional blue and white railing, cemented deck, with your typical tackle shop and cafe on the end looking out toward Catalina's faint outline across the bright blue water. Ah, but today it's khaki-colored inshore and for almost a mile out, a separate stream clearly marking the outflow from the Santa Ana River mouth upcoast after the rainstorm two days ago. A scalloped line of inland refuse marks

Dorymen have been bringing in their catch to sell beside Newport Pier for the last hundred years. Scales are hung on an oar.

the high tide line, palm fronds and plastic artifacts, oranges and lemons and tennis balls.

Alongside the pier is the dory fishermen's layout...a link with the past. The only such operation on the West Coast, the dorymen have been part of Newport as long as the pier itself. Since the 1890s they've launched their open boats every day, weather permitting, leaving well before dawn to bring their catch back through the breakers to the waiting customers. Boat beached, the fisherman hauls out his portable fish-cleaning sink, drives an oar in the sand to hang up the scales, and gets out his knife and sharpening stone, cleaning the fish to your order on the spot.

These days the dorymen use outboards instead of oars to push their fourteen-foot boats through the surf, and a pickup truck with four-wheel drive pulls them up the beach, where once the customers pitched in to help roll the boat up the sand a few feet at a time, taking up the rear log and putting it under the bow. And the fishing tackle goes into big locked boxes. "Nowadays even another fisherman will steal your stuff," said doryman Luke Pangle. "Not like the old days."

But their way of life is like the old days, when an individual's very survival could depend strictly on his own skills. It's an uncertain economic life, too—no regular wages, and none of those benefits—reflecting an independence not seen much nowadays. Even so, it's attracted several young fishermen, meaning that the tradition may endure a little longer.

The oldest pier on the south coast, McFadden's Wharf was built in 1888 to accommodate the trains that ran out here from Santa Ana every day but Sunday, bringing grain, local produce and passengers who boarded the schooners and steamships which tied up here. This particular spot was chosen for the wharf because rowers had discovered a calm area offshore, above a submarine canyon.

The Santa Ana & Newport ran one train a day in winter, three daily in summer plus excursions, moving as many as fifty cars a day onto the 1,300-foot wharf, then wide enough on the end to hold six tracks side by side.

Henry Huntington, who in 1904 had bought into the company developing the Balboa Peninsula, brought his trolley line on down the coast to Newport in 1905. Southern Pacific had already bought out the local railroad, and in 1907 they shut it down entirely to eliminate competition with their Long Wharf at Santa Monica; but the wharf at Newport had already become the center of a community.

Local waters were incredibly rich, and fishermen in small boats dropped their nets around schools of smelt and then used teams of horses to haul their catches onto the beach, three or four tons at a time. In the '20s and '30s, when pier fishing was still done with cane poles, schools of mackerel, white sea bass and barracuda used to come in under the pier.

"You'd see a hundred cane poles all bend at once when the mackerel hit," said long-time doryman Pangle. "We fished black sea bass off the beach then...sometimes you'd see twenty on the beach at one time. We'd carry them up on stretchers and roll them over onto the cutting planks."

While the storms of '83 did no harm to this pier, oldtimers remember the last "really big one." On September 24, 1939, following nine days of 100-degree-plus temperatures, a tropical hurricane swept in with winds recorded at San Pedro at Force 11—Force 10 on the Beaufort scale is a whole gale, Force 11 a storm with winds 55-62 mph and exceptionally high waves. Seas were twelve to fifteen feet high inside the outer harbor at San Pedro, and waves in the open ocean reached thirty to forty-five feet.

With high tide over five feet, peninsula streets were flooded by the surf; the dorymen tied their boats to lamp-posts on the inside of the street, and waves running thirty feet high destroyed the last 400 feet of the pier.

Rebuilt the following year to 1,032 feet, the pier reopened with a gigantic fish fry at which 20,000 people reportedly did away with three tons of fish.

The pier today is a cosmopolitan place: in a single circuit of the T end you may hear Japanese, Spanish, German, Samoan, Arabic...little enclaves each speaking their own language, fishing their own way. Something new: several Vietnamese with cane poles tipped with cloth or leather instead of the usual metal, reeling up the line on a big cardboard spool, endlessly turning as they troll their bait.

The small submarine canyon approaches the head of the pier, so that within 600 feet the water is 100 feet deep or more. Lively and varied fishing here sometimes includes squid, caught at night when the lights attract them: in 1976 a big run of giant squid brought Oriental fishermen on the run to catch this delicacy. And in the summer of '78, a fifteen-year-old hauled in an eight-foot hammerhead shark weighing 225 pounds.

From the deck up on top of the cafe you get an admiral's eye view of the pier, surfers riding the breakers, Balboa Pier two miles downcoast. The shining towers inland to the right are the bank buildings and dentists' offices of Newport Center, on the mainland.

Days when the flags on the lifeguard station are snapping in the wind, you can locate the foot of the pier even before you get there by the crowd of seagulls overhead, hovering in position above the beached dories, waiting to get the leavings of the day's catch.

"I put two hundred pounds of fish guts down there in the surf one day: we weighed it," said a tattooed doryman. "And do you know how long it took the seagulls to clean them all up? By my watch—four minutes."

Huntington Beach Pier without its landmark "The End Cafe."

HUNTINGTON BEACH PIER

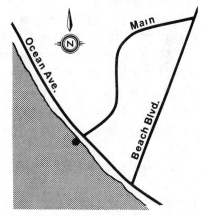

Huntington. Every surfer in Southern California knows it. Summer and winter the craggy old pier witnesses them, the sub-teenagers watching and waiting, thrashing into position to catch their first waves, and the veterans riding the crest, sometimes even cutting through the barnacle-crusted pilings and shooting out the other side.

There's something faintly medieval about the 1,800-foot pier. Its tall concrete pilings, the color and texture of wet sand, fan out to support the central platform and a pair of outsets holding the little snack shops buttressed like watchtowers. Just beyond them a futuristic lifeguard tower looms over everything, its windows slanting outward to the overhanging roof so that the lounging lifeguard is on display, sneakers and all.

The pier is an extension of Main Street, and that's what it feels like, drawing strollers and fishermen at all hours. The Tackle Box, the Captain's Galley, where you can get chowder and hamburgers, and Neptune's Locker, with beer and sandwiches and a color TV next to the window with its panoramic view, and stools made from pieces of old light poles, are all three run by Ella Christensen, 70, who's been here almost continually since 1951.

She opens the Tackle Box at 6:00 A.M. and closes Neptune at 1:00 A.M. "What you want to poison yourself with them things for?" she says to a young man buying a pack of cigarettes. Some call her the Queen of the Pier: she's hired a couple of generations of local kids to sell bait and flip hamburgers, knows everybody, and keeps proceedings on an even keel out here.

In the storms of January-March '83, the End Cafe and the end of the pier itself were badly battered by the big waves, and had to be torn out and rebuilt. During the height of the final storm the beachfront was jammed with despairing watchers as the pier's deck began to break away.

But unlike officials in most other coastal cities, when the city's insurance man purchased a $2.5 million policy for the pier, he took it upon himself to spend $3,500 on special wave damage coverage. In view of the estimated $260,000 needed to repair the pier, it was a real bargain.

It wasn't the first time the pier's been damaged, of course. A pier has stood on this spot since 1903, when the infant town was named Pacific City in hopes that it would become the western equivalent of Atlantic City. In 1930 a 500-foot wooden extension added to it was built four feet lower by mistake—the inclined section connected the two parts is clearly evident, about two-thirds of the way out—and this difference in elevation apparently made the pier more vulnerable to heavy seas.

The 1933 earthquake popped the two sections apart. The gap was patched over again, but in September '39 a tropical hurricane sweeping up the coast smashed the end of the pier, which held a heavy six-sided sunroom. At the height of the storm, giant green swells rolled over the end, breaking out the sunroom's windows, and by nightfall the whole end was torn away, including the two outermost T's you see today.

Repaired once more, the pier's status changed abruptly on December 7, 1941, the morning that Pearl Harbor was bombed. Fearing that an invasion by the Japanese was imminent, the Army occupied "Huntington" for the duration of the war, installing an Army radio station, radar and a searchlight, and machine gun emplacements on the outer end standing ready to repel the invader.

Huntington's flat, sandy bottom has made for good surfing since the beginning. At the foot of the pier on a chunk of lava, a bronze bust of Duke Kahanamoku, his broad Polynesian nose kept polished bright by affectionate hands, salutes his contribution to the place and the sport. A champion swimmer and later a four-time Olympic winner, the twenty-year-old Hawaiian helped introduce surfing here when he visited Southern California in 1911 on his way to the 1912 Olympics. He and his fellow Hawaiian, George Freeth, surfed several local beaches.

Huntington resident Bud Higgins, a former captain of lifeguards here, got interested in surfing during the '20s, when he and a friend who'd seen the surfing in Hawaii decided to design and build their own boards.

Of solid redwood, the boards were ten feet long and weighed around 135 pounds. "All the kids on the beach learned to surf on those boards," Higgins said. "They were the only ones around." Periodically the boards got waterlogged and had to be dried out and re-varnished. And they were dangerous when they got away from the surfer—head injuries were not uncommon. In contrast, today's fiberglassed boards weigh around ten pounds; and most surfers use a "kook cord" tethering the board to an ankle or wrist to keep from having to chase it.

The first West Coast Surfing Championships were held here in 1959, becoming the U.S. Surfing Championships in 1968. A yearly Huck Finn—Becky Thatcher Day is held on the pier itself in July, a kids' contest with prizes for costumes and the best catches. With rollerskate rentals, the inevitable video arcade, biking, and K-runs periodically held on the beach path from Newport Beach, there's always plenty to do.

At night the Golden Bear, just across Pacific Coast Highway, holds concerts with such name rock, folk and blues musicians as Richie Havens, Joe Turner and Tower of Power. At the foot of the pier there's a ticket office for other Southern California entertainment, and a pizza place with a couple of outside tables. And a block down the highway is a shiny silver Amtrak car filled with railroad mementos, the Chew Chew Cafe.

Upcoast several drilling platforms tap the tidelands oil pool. Oil was discovered here in 1920, when Bolsa Chica #1 came in, and the practice of whip-stocking, or slant drilling, also originated here in 1932, with hundreds of wells driven at an angle under the ocean's bottom for more than a mile to tap the submarine oil. You can see the grasshopper-shaped pumps working all along the westward bluff: more of them are scattered around town, pumping away in back yards and empty lots.

From the end of the pier you can see Catalina dead ahead, when it's clear enough. One clear summer Sunday morning, dozens of surfers plunged into the surf wearing flower leis, paddled out one-handed with bunches of flowers carefully balanced in front of them on their boards.

They gathered in a great ring off the end of the pier, a hundred or so rocking on their boards and holding hands, surrounding a brilliant mass of floating flowers. One of the surfers circled inside the ring on his board, keeping the flowers together, while up on the pier another cluster of people gathered around the minister who was conducting the memorial service for his father.

At sunset they're still coming and going—families with sleepy kids, taking them home after a day's fishing, replaced by others just coming out, bouncing and bright-eyed. Lovers and after-dinner strollers in the fading light...the big flared lamps come on, pale greenish at first and making everyone look ghastly for a few moments. A half-grown boy leans far out, legs locked around the railing, his hand line wrapped onto a flattened soft drink can, jerking it with little calculated twitches. And down below a few diehard surfers are still at it, riding their boards by pier-light.

SEAL BEACH PIER

Well-covered beachgoers promenade at the entrance to Seal Beach Pier on a hazy afternoon during World War I. Fireworks were shot off Nighly from the tower out on the end of the pier.

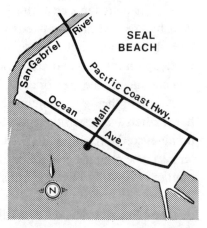

Seal Beach announces its presence by those rows of tall, skinny pom-pom palms bending in concert, sure sign of an old-timey California community. The little town is flat as a table, and Seal Beach Pier shoots out dead level with recently renovated Main Street and its trim shops and bricked intersections. From the foot of the pier you see the downcoast beach piled high with sand, while the upcoast beach is low, flat and oil-stained. Ocean currents deflected by the Long Beach Harbor breakwater cut in here and carry sand away, and only the concrete seawall down the right side of the pier keeps the pier pilings from being undermined.

The jetty downcoast protects the entrance to Alamitos Bay, now a U.S. Navy facility; and the man-made island off the end of the pier holds California's first offshore oil well, drilled in 1954. Upcoast you see the Long Beach skyline with arching Vincent Thomas Bridge and the San Pedro headlands beyond. The sea hereabouts is usually filled with the traffic of cargo ships and pleasure boats moving in and out of the harbor.

At 1,865 feet, the pier is one of the longest on the coast, and its continued existence is a tribute to the energies of local residents. In the mighty storms of January 1983, two chunks were torn away: the first of March, the rest of the center section went, leaving the end with its tackle and ticket building, live bait tank and cafe (the "Seal Beach Grand Old Opry House") a marooned and forlorn island. Residents vowed to raise the town's twenty-five percent share of the $2.5 million needed to rebuild the pier—and succeeded; with the grand re-opening on Labor Day 1984.

Maybe they were heartened by the pier's revival after an earlier disaster. Seal Beach Pier weathered both the '33 earthquake and the '39 hurricane undamaged: its moment of crisis came on a summer night in 1935.

Big breakers, driven by a distant storm, were pounding the beach; but the balmy evening had brought out plenty of strollers, and fishing was fine out on the end. Then, without apparent warning, the pier broke in two. The break was fairly close to shore, and twenty people were stranded on the outer end, their rescue complicated by a powerful high tide at 7:45. The Coast Guard came to the rescue, rigging a bosun's chair to lift each one across. Last off were the unruffled fishermen, reluctant to tear themselves away from the "really good fishing."

Built in 1906, the pier became the heart of the "Jewel City" amusement resort, with a roller coaster shipped down from the San Francisco Fair along with fifty giant scintillator lamps which cast changing rainbows on the water for night bathing.

Stunt flying and movie stars helped draw the crowds, but not everybody approved: an Orange County minister denounced the town as "The Plague Spot at Our Doors." Although women bathers were still required to wear stockings, elsewhere some daring souls were already rolling them down to just below the knee. "But at Seal Beach," a reporter wrote in 1916, "girls are painting their legs to fool the coppers."

BELMONT PIER

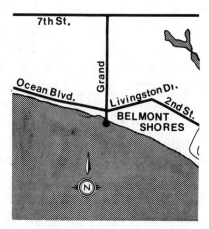

Belmont Pier lies within the shelter of the Long Beach Harbor breakwater, so that the surf on the flat, sandy beach here is only a gentle sigh. If you've never seen one of the big new piers, you're in for a surprise. All sharp strokes, concrete and metal lamps and its Y arms angled wide, on that foggy no-color day it looked like an architect's drawing brought to life.

A floating boat dock slants in to the left arm of the Y, and as it rocks on the surf you hear the shriek of metal against metal. Upcoast the Queen Mary lies at anchor off Long Beach, with its three fat slanted orange stacks, black-tipped, a noted landmark. This side of the ship a white dome seems to be resting on the water...it's the new home of Howard Hughes' wooden flying boat, the *Spruce Goose*.

Belmont is a serious fishing pier, in use twenty-four hours a day. Along the main stem, several boys fished with a wooden sinker like a length of dowel, with three hooks attached and little tags fluttering on each; continually casting out and reeling in bursts, to catch the fishes' attention. Seagulls hung around one of the concrete sinks waiting while a man from the Louisiana bayous cleaned his catch of bonita. He didn't care for them, he said, but his wife liked them: he preferred catfish.

You can also take a half-day or three-quarter-day sportfishing boat here, or go out to the 150-foot fishing barge, the *Annie B*, anchored inside the breakwater: it's open Friday morning to Sunday afternoon.

The two-story building centering the end of the pier has a tackle stand which sells live bait, and a lifeguard station upstairs, facing the shore. Around on the sea side the snack bar, with three outside tables and benches sheltered by a windbreak, is open every day.

The 1,450-foot pier was constructed for $1.5 million, part of Long Beach's tidelands oil income. It was built in 1967 alongside the original wooden pier, which was torn down. That pier had been opened on Christmas Day, 1915—it was often called Devil's Gate Pier because of a natural bridge (since eroded away) which extended from the low bluff. At low tide, residents could walk or ride their horses through Devil's Gate.

All of Belmont Shores was just tidal flats then, until two million cubic yards of sand were pumped from Alamitos Bay onto the plain. Developers sold the first lot here in 1920. That same year, the little town held a bond election to buy this beach from its private owners for $37.50 a front foot, because developers wanted to put a mile of highway 100 feet wide down the beach. After a bitter campaign, the bonds were defeated: but the highway was later re-routed inland, and the city eventually bought the beach—for $175-$200 a front foot.

The neighborhood around the pier is quiet, mostly residential, but you'll find a couple of fast food places up on Ocean Avenue. The big building beyond the parking lot is a five-story swimming complex, built in 1968 for $3.7 million, which was also tidelands oil money. It houses an Olympic swimming pool where coaches can watch their swimmers from an underwater viewing room, and give them instructions at poolside via underwater speakers. Reportedly the third largest swimming pool complex in the world, it can accommodate 2,500-3,000 spectators.

Sunset today is a yellow haze, silhouetting the oil drilling islands to the right of the pier and off the end, their pumps hidden by futuristic rectangles and globes. Some families head home, while others are just arriving for their Friday night outing, with paper sacks of food and sleeping bags for the little ones.

Night fishing is a little different here. There are electric outlets at intervals along the pier, and several fishermen have drop-lights on long plastic cords hanging just above the surface. Through the greenish water, patches of anchovies move and turn all at once, like bits of silver metal magnetized. From the depths the larger fish rise and materialize for a moment and then dissolve.

Along the wall of the restroom building at the wide spot halfway out, several children are going to sleep. A little Mexican girl with her bottle strokes her head and hums to herself while a few feet away her parents, fishing near someone's light, haul in the perch. Out on the lefthand Y end a party of Orientals has a run of good-sized bonita, reeling them in and swinging them onto the pier as fast as they can. A school of larger fish out here under the light, perch, maybe, hang around ignoring the fuss, continually moving shadows that maintain a constant distance between themselves, always about a foot apart.

It's a warm October night, and the third game of the World Series is on: the portable radios and the open windows in the condominium back of the parking lot all speak with a single voice. The drilling island alongside is fantastical, two towers with rows of greenish lights, big globes of yellow and orange glowing; and the surf slaps on the dark-streaked sand. Oil.

CABRILLO PIER

Lying just inside the Los Angeles Harbor Breakwater, Cabrillo Pier provides a ringside seat on one of the world's great seaports. You approach it from the foot of the bluff, where a sand spit anchors the two-mile upcoast arm of the breakwater. Back here is a tree-shaded park with barbecues and playground equipment, a cafe where you can buy beer with your food, and a parking lot; or you can park outside on the street and walk down.

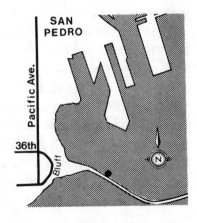

A quarter-mile out on the spit is another parking lot which serves the pier. Dedicated in 1969, Cabrillo lies parallel to the breakwater, where a two-language sign warns of *Oleaje Peligroso*—Dangerous Waves—which sometimes catch fishermen on the rocks unawares. But the pier itself is sheltered, and offers a constantly changing panorama.

Today the black-and-red oil tankers and the giant container ship *Silver Longevity,* with its white cargo booms, dwarf an elegant white cruise ship on her way to Panama and the Caribbean. Just opposite on Terminal Island in 1977 the *Sansinena* exploded amidships and cracked in two, the concussion shattering windows up the hillsides.

When Richard Henry Dana stopped here on the brig *Pilgrim* in 1835, San Pedro was already the California seaport shipping the most hides. This rocky point was Sepulveda's Landing then, part of the Rancho Sepulveda: the first pier, Tomlinson's Wharf, was built here sometime before 1850. It being mostly destroyed in an 1858 storm, that energetic pioneer Phineas Banning moved around to the mud flats opposite, which were better protected, and built another wharf at a spot he named Wilmington, after his birthplace.

Terminal Island was then known as Rattlesnake Island because of the number of beasts which washed down from the San Gabriel Mountains in the winter rains and congregated there. Nevertheless it became a vacation spot, location of the little town of Brighton Beach, which had its own pleasure pier. And out in the center of the channel a large chunk of rock stuck up, Dead Man's Island.

The region already needed a harbor, and in 1871 the U.S. government built a breakwater from Rattlesnake to Dead Man's Island, creating a current which scoured the channel, and then dredged to further deepen the channel. Along this breakwater a shack colony of squatters, fishermen and vacationers sprang up, among them writer Charles Lummis, who described fishing for his dinner as he worked. He kept a fishing line strung out the back door and fastened by a bed-spring to a cowbell, so that it would ring when he got a strike.

Harbor facilities were hardly adequate to the growing demands of landlocked Los Angeles, twenty miles from the coast. Three towns vied for the rich future awaiting L.A.'s seaport—Santa Monica, Redondo Beach and San Pedro; but none of them was naturally sheltered, and an extensive breakwater would be the vital first step. Collis Huntington, whose Southern Pacific Railway had a monopoly at Santa Monica, labored to persuade the U.S. Congress to accept his choice: but other interests prevailed, and Senator Stephen White finally secured the harbor funds for San Pedro after a climactic three-day Congressional debate.

Several more years passed before the money was pried loose and bids actually let for the long-awaited breakwater. San Pedro and Los Angeles prepared to match White's debate with a three-day celebration to commemorate the start of the breakwater. On April 26, 1899, President McKinley in the White House flashed the signal to drop the first rock, using a solid gold telegraph key. Cannons fired, skyrockets went up, and the crowds cheered as the first boulder was levered off the barge and plunged into the water. Alas—the rock floated: it was pumice.

While this two-mile breakwater was abuilding, Los Angeles annexed a shoestring strip, sixteen miles long and a mile wide, which connected it to San Pedro and Wilmington, and then annexed the two towns. Los Angeles finally had its harbor.

The harbor lighthouse out on the end of the breakwater has been a landmark since 1913. Built on a concrete block forty feet square, the two bottom stories are covered with steel plates, and the upper stories are of cement on structural steel. During its early years a severe gale knocked it out of line, giving it a slight shoreward tilt.

Its exposed situation subjects it to high seas which sometimes maroon the lighthouse keeper: windows thirty-five feet above the sea have been smashed, and salt water has reached to the top of the seventy-three-foot tower. On a few occasions the fuel supply gave out and the keeper, unable to reach the storage building thirty feet away, had to cook his dinner with a blowtorch. The lighthouse is now equipped with a fourth order bivalve lens, a diaphragm fog signal and a radio beacon.

President Teddy Roosevelt, already a local hero because of his support of the Panama Canal (a great boon to West Coast shipping), sent the sixteen ships of the Great White Fleet steaming into the harbor in 1908 on their round-the-world cruise. Four of them anchored inside the new breakwater, and the local citizenry climbed aboard to tour them.

The discovery in 1921 of oil at Signal Hill, just south of Long Beach, produced a local boom. The close-packed wells were soon producing almost 250,000 barrels a day; the population of Long Beach tripled, and the volume of shipping through the Panama Canal doubled.

Prohibition brought smuggling to the coast, with big "mother ships" lying safely outside the twelve-mile limit waiting to turn over their cases of Scotch to the twenty-knot cutters which, running at night and without lights, could easily outrun the Coast Guard's twelve-knot vessels. Bootleggers dropped their cargoes at a number of spots well-known in local folklore, including Dead Man's island—until it was pronounced a shipping hazard, and dynamited and removed in 1929.

The 12,500-foot detached center section of the breakwater, begun in 1932, further increased the harbor's capacity. Despite its great volume of shipping during World War II, the harbor's worst disaster didn't occur till afterwards, in 1947, when tanks #3 and #7 aboard the oil tanker *Markay* blew up at Shell Oil's Berth 168. The *Markay* held 35,000 barrels of oil: eleven people were killed and twenty-two others injured in the explosion and fire which followed.

Today's container ships dwarf the *Markay*...in fact, oldtimers say that the harbor seems less busy than in the past, although the volume of cargo continues to increase, because of the new ships' immense capacity.

Pollution, once a problem in the harbor, has lessened, and fishermen here now catch kelp and sand bass, bonita, perch and occasionally a halibut. The orange-roofed building on the pier houses both a snack stand and a tackle stand with live bait and poles for rent, both open seven days a week. Its service windows, which face across the breakwater into the prevailing wind, are shielded by heavy clear plastic with a two-inch-square hole cut out for conversation.

Skindivers take rock scallops and sometimes a lobster on the outside of the breakwater, and there's also good hunting around the rocky shoreline of the point. Some of us can remember wading in the pools at White's Point on a minus tide when you could still find abalone big enough to keep.

Waves on the ocean side at Cabrillo provide some surfing. The larger beach inside the bay was created by the tons of sand dredged from the harbor channel, and you can rent wind-surfers here.

The light grey building behind the bay beach is the new Cabrillo Marine Museum, with whalebones to climb over in the courtyard, a whale room inside with a huge skeleton, and tanks where you can get nose to nose with marvelous sea-creatures—moray eels, huge many-legged starfish covered with pink fuzz, a baby shark, dancing octopus, and the fantastic inch-long Spanish Shawl, flaming purple with orange fringe waving along its back. The museum is open daily except Mondays, Thanksgiving and Christmas: don't miss it.

In the afternoon an onshore wind often comes up, sweeping across from the point to power the sailboats, many with bright-striped balloon jibs. The sun moving westward puts the park in the shade while the pier still has hours of sunlight.

It's a peaceful family pier...a young black father teaching his son to fish says, "Now, don't rest the pole on the rail: you hold the pole in your hand." A two-masted sailboat skims past, heading in before the wind dies. And then just at dusk the lighthouse at the end of the breakwater comes on, showing sailors of craft large and small the way to their berths.

REDONDO PIERS KING HARBOR

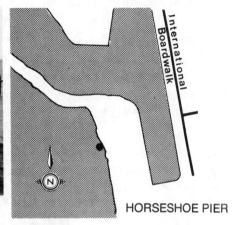

HORSESHOE PIER

(Above) Original Horseshoe Pier, built in 1915;
(Below) South side of today's Monstad Pier.

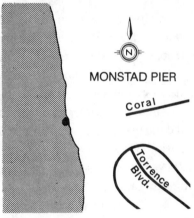

MONSTAD PIER

Coral

Torrence Blvd.

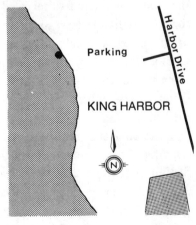

Parking

Harbor Drive

KING HARBOR

Today the Southern California pier which begins to compare with the great old amusement piers of Santa Monica Bay is Redondo Beach—actually three piers; the horseshoe Municipal Pier, Monstad Pier which shares its land approach, and the new fishing pier to the north, sheltered by the King Harbor breakwater.

The piers house a clutch of restaurants, most with satisfying views; curio, clothing and kite shops, fish markets, pastry, sausage, balloons, salt-water taffy, stands where you can get clam chowder at an outdoor table, pearls, posters and two jazz spots.

On the ocean front inside the horseshoe, in the bottom level of the parking structure, the Fun Zone has video games and shooting galleries, bumper cars and table hockey. Alongside it is another block of shops and quick food stands, including Indonesian and African, and a big fish market with rock scallops, oysters, mussels, sea urchins and several varieties of clam, all alive, and crabs and lobsters you can have cooked while you wait. Round cement outdoor tables are spread with newspapers, and you can get beer and a lobster, check out a nutcracker and have an *al fresco* feast.

You can fish on the breakwater or any of the piers—there's live bait on the end of Monstad, where most of the fishermen congregate. Harbor cruises are announced over loudspeakers; or you can just walk out on the jetty and watch the passing boats. The blossoming of Redondo Pier came along with the area's redevelopment and the building of the harbor, which Redondoans had yearned for since 1890.

Redondo was born in the 1880s land boom, when diligent advertising and a railway rate war brought a rush of people to Southern California—for a while in 1886, you could ride from the Midwest to Los Angeles for $1. Crowds were lured to Redondo Beach and other new developments with barbeques, band music, and plenty of free beer and whisky.

The town's career as a seaport began in 1890, when Wharf No. 1 was finished and the first coastal steamer docked here. Wharf No. 2 followed in 1895, a curving Y with one side for pedestrians and fishermen and the other for the Santa Fe Railway tracks, so that incoming lumber and other goods could be unloaded directly onto the train cars.

The two arms converged 300 feet out and extended another 175 feet. Study of the ocean floor here had revealed a deep submarine canyon which curves in close to shore, so that large vessels could easily approach a short dock. This was a prime argument of Redondo promoters, who yearned to provide the harbor which landlocked Los Angeles was seeking. So did San Pedro and Santa Monica: and all three were open roadsteads. Ships at Redondo were exposed to eight points of the compass, and in heavy seas more than one was driven aground and broke up on the beach.

That same submarine canyon which brought shipping to Redondo made the building of a large offshore breakwater impossible. Promoters even suggested a floating breakwater across the heart of the submarine canyon. Not feasible, the Army Engineers decided; and Redondo lost out. Another shipping pier was built in 1903, and 600 ships docked at Redondo at 1904 alone: but, as San Pedro's shipping grew, Redondo's shrank.

Henry Huntington and his Pacific Electric Railway saved the town, by turning it into a tourist attraction. In fact, when Huntington bought into the town in 1905, he precipitated another land boom. More than a hundred real estate offices set up on the waterfront, many in tents. Railway conductors were buying lots in Redondo and selling them to passengers on the next trip...one house, it's recorded, sold for $4,000 in the morning, was resold for $10,000 before noon, and again for $20,000 by nightfall.

The elegant Hotel Redondo, built in 1891 on the knoll just south of the pier where the town library now stands, was the sister of San Diego's Hotel Del Coronado, and had an eighteen-hole golf course and a grand ballroom overlooking the busy harbor. On the Midway at the foot of the pier Huntington built a saltwater plunge, a casino seating 1,200, and the Mandarin Pavilion, where patrons could hear band concerts, and later on, that strange, new jazz music.

In 1907 Huntington brought George Freeth over from the Hawaiian Islands as aquatic director to help promote "the biggest salt-water plunge in the world." Freeth, Irish and Hawaiian, and others had revived the ancient Hawaiian sport of board surfing. Writer Jack London, cruising the Pacific in his *Snark*, was in the surf off Waikiki trying to learn "the royal sport" when, he wrote, "one Freeth" appeared on his board. "I saw him tearing in on the back of it, standing upright on his board, carelessly poised, a young god bronzed with sunburn."

Freeth became the first lifeguard on the West Coast, and introduced the sport of Polynesian nobility to California, riding the Redondo breakers on an eight-foot board of solid wood that weighed 200 pounds. He was accordingly billed as "the man who could walk on water."

You'll find a bronze bust of George Freeth on a boulder where the south leg of the horseshoe pier meets the shoreline. Best surfing nowadays is evidently well south of the pier, down toward Torrance Beach, although some experienced surfers ride the winter swells outside the breakwater.

With the help of the Pacific Electric Railway, Redondo became the Big Red Car Resort. In 1909 the trolleys carried 934,000 passengers; the next year, 2,020,000. Redondo's Midway, now more elegantly named El Paseo, by 1913 included a theater, bowling alleys, a Hippodrome and the Great White Lightning Roller Coaster; and in 1915 the Endless Pier, shaped very like today's horseshoe, was built of concrete and steel, a modern marvel.

A storm shortly destroyed the roller coaster, which was rebuilt at once, and damaged the Endless Pier, which deteriorated till '29, when it was properly rebuilt of wood, as you see it today. The Hotel Redondo didn't survive. Declared too expensive to operate, it was boarded up, and in 1925 was demolished and its lumber sold for $200.

Monstad Pier, which shares its landward approach with the horseshoe pier, was built in 1927 by Capt. W.M. Monstad, a former merchant marine skipper, as a fishing pier and dock for his sport-fishing boats. From the pier in the '20s and '30s, water taxis carried passengers out to the *Tango* and other gambling ships anchored beyond the three-mile limit. For a really big evening during the Depression, you could spend 25¢ on the water taxi, go out for the free buffet, and maybe spend a couple of dollars gambling.

During the '30s gambling sprouted on El Paseo, too, with chip games and bingo parlors. When bingo was declared a "game of chance" and outlawed, operators re-named it *tango, beano* or *corno*, and customers took turns throwing a little ball on a board to make it land on a desired number; which clearly made it a "game of skill."

And the Wagon Wheel, open in '39 and '40, was a private gambling club complete with a guard watching behind a one-way mirror and armed with a shotgun. Underworld figures from elsewhere were seen about town: in 1937 one of them, George Bruneman, was shot in the back as he strolled along El Paseo with his girlfriend. Bruneman survived the shooting, only to be killed later in a Sunset Strip night club.

In 1940 P.E. abandoned its streetcar line into Redondo and the amusement zone it had operated since 1914, and the piers languished.

Their revival coincided with the building of the small boat harbor and the mile-long breakwater which were finished in 1958, after several years of problems. The first breakwater built was much shorter, but it cut off the flow of sand and caused waves to converge north of Redondo Canyon, which undermined the Boardwalk and buildings behind, destroying a whole block including the old Fox Theater. To correct the situation Army Engineers had to extend the breakwater to he southeast, and add the jetty beside the horseshoe pier. But Redondoans finally got their harbor, after seventy years of yearning.

The massive redevelopment project which accompanied the building of the harbor obliterated El Paseo and Redondo's downtown, replacing it with fifty acres of high-rise apartments which overlook piers and harbor and wall off the town behind, leaving those of us who remember the "real" Redondo feeling forever displaced and muttering.

The marina next door also has restaurants and several public tennis and raquetball courts, and a 250-foot fishing pier opened in 1970, where you can get tickets for half-day and all-day boats or whale-watching trips during the winter migration of the California grey whale. Fishing from the pier is free. We saw larger bonita being brought in here than anywhere else, and yellowtail is also caught from this pier.

A permanent boil just south of this pier marks the outlet from the Southern California Edison generating station just behind the harbor. Some fishermen believe that its warmer water attracts fish. In November 1978 about 500 yellowtail washed ashore in this area, evidently killed by a chlorine discharge from the Edison plant.

Irresistible progress continues to transform the place. On top of the parking structure, a spot with a commanding view of pier and harbor, another shopping complex has just been built—one more mock New England whaling village. (Naturally—nothing in California's heritage worth remembering.) Residents in the apartments behind protested fruitlessly that their view would be destroyed.

Out on the pier the salt air and sea fogs are softening the gloss of the new buildings, and another decade or so of humanity, French fries with vinegar, cut bait and pigeons should effectively mellow the place. There are still several corners where you can lean or sit and watch the sea surge through the pilings, and the sailboats catching a breeze. In an outside angle, three young boys in face masks and wetsuit tops are diving for coins, storing them in their mouths.

Looking across to Monstad, you can see a pronounced sag in the deck line. The restaurant next to the bait stand has been closed, and the city-owned pier is in definite need of repair. For forty years this has been a favorite fishing spot: you can get live bait here, and the best halibut hole around is along the south side of the pier, where that submarine canyon comes close in and the water is fifty-sixty feet deep.

One day several years back, fishermen on Monstad discovered that they had to let out more and more line to hit bottom. Within two hours the water had deepened by about twenty feet, caused by the sand flowing away into the canyon, and the pier became very unstable. Fortunately, the waves soon deposited fresh sand around the pilings.

The current pier lessee, Tony Trutanich, has been wanting to remodel this pier and build a restaurant, move the bait boat landing 100 feet inland, and relocate fishermen to a new cross-section which would be built linking the end of Monstad with the horseshoe pier. Fishermen protested and set about collecting signatures to petition the Coastal Commission. Said one, "You can put a restaurant anyplace; but you can only catch fish in the ocean."

HERMOSA PIER

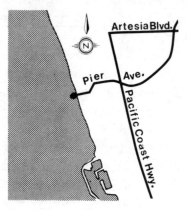

Since its beginning seventy-five years and three piers ago, Hermosa has always been a fishing pier, where fisher-children as young as eight or nine come down alone and in bunches to spend the day catching smelt, mackerel and half-moon or opal eye perch. They get dead bait from the old man who runs the snack stand, and trade off using a grappling anchor to pull mussels off the pilings for bait—it's a cone-shaped arrangement of metal rods pointing up, lowered on the end of a rope: they pull it up under the mussels, and pry them loose.

From the foot of Pier Avenue all you see of the pier is a wide concrete vestibule with built-in benches, and the rising ramp of the pier, concealing the rest of it. Trim and no-nonsense, the entrance would be bleak without the presence of people. Having no outsets and few benches make the pier seem longer than its 1,140 feet. Although it's fifty feet above the ocean floor out here and twenty-four feet above the water, "I've seen waves breaking over the end," the old man says. "Shaking the pier, poles in the rack rolling back and forth—when you've got high winds and a high tide, you get wet out here."

But today is sunny and calm. Off the El Segundo oil pier upcoast two oil tankers are anchored, one red below and black above, and powerboats from King Harbor just downcoast trail their white-ruffle wakes across the blue water. And if the fish aren't biting, there's plenty more to do: it's a flat, sandy beach with volleyball nets alongside, and good swimming and surfing. Beside the two-story lifeguard station on the pier's south edge is a blackboard showing the day's high and low tides, air and water temperature, surfing conditions: "Surf one to two feet; rip-tides present."

Along the wide concrete boardwalk are several bike and roller-skate rentals, and the first block of Pier Avenue is also tuned to the youth trade. Outside the Mermaid's Rest, a seafood restaurant at the foot of the pier, the rusty bike-rack is half full. On the south side of the pier the Lighthouse has come and gone—and may be back by now: who knows? It was a jazz spot for more than thirty years, since that Sunday afternoon in the late forties when the then-owner was persuaded by Howard Rumsey to offer live jazz here. In the years since, Chico Hamilton, Shelley Manne and a host of other West Coast jazz figures passed through. Up on the corner of Hermosa and Pier avenues, Shenanigans, a big sandwich-and place, features rock groups; another sign of the times.

For years the double tracks of the Pacific Electric Railway and its Big Red Cars ran along Hermosa Avenue. In 1904 the street was paved, and the first pier and the two-mile boardwalk were both built. As in Manhattan, the town fathers wanted Hermosa to be strictly a family community, and so refused to allow any amusements.

By 1913 that pier was badly battered, and the concrete structure which replaced it had an auditorium on its landward end, used for meetings and cultural activities, including the town library. William Jennings Bryan spent several summers here in his later years, a familiar sight fishing in his overalls and an old straw hat and conversing with the other pier regulars.

This pier, too, gradually succumbed to winter storms and was condemned and demolished. The city bought the strip of beach 210 feet on either side of the pier for $250,000, and the city and the California Wildlife Commission went halves on the present pier, which cost around $600,000 and was finished in 1965.

The statue of a surfer you see at the entrance is dedicated to Tim Kelley, a local lifeguard who was killed at twenty-four in a car accident: it was moved up from Tim Kelley Beach in south Redondo. "We gave permission to put it up here," said Marty DeMott, Hermosa recreation director, "because people always think of Hermosa and surfing together."

MANHATTAN BEACH PIER

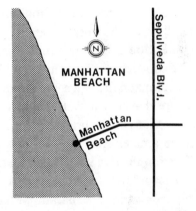

As you come over the last rise and down the hill, Manhattan Beach Pier stretches out dead ahead from the foot of the street. Crowning its straight stem and round end is a faded blue pavilion, octagonal, with arched windows and a roof of tiles painted red, the whole tranquil and mildly Mediterranean in flavor.

After long years of silence the pavilion has come to life again, with tackle and fast food resident. The pier draws both local aficionados and inlanders from Lawndale, north Redondo and Hawthorne, who get perch and smelt, and sometimes a barracuda.

The beach here, long considered one of the best swimming beaches in Southern California, is much wider now than when the pier was built, thanks to Redondo's breakwater which slows the current and causes sand to deposit at Manhattan and Hermosa. Surfers near the pier sometimes find the breakers short, steep and twisting, requiring much skill to ride. Manhattan and Hermosa together have five miles of good surf, ridable all year round.

Opened in 1920, the pier was given its round end so that wave action wouldn't hit all the pilings at the same time—the previous pier at this spot having been demolished by a storm in 1913.

That first pier, built in 1900, was called the Old Iron Pier because its pilings were made by bundling three railroad ties together and driving them into the ocean floor. One of the hazards in jumping off the present pier is the possibility of lighting on a jagged remnant of an original piling.

Alongside the Old Iron Pier a wave machine was put in, one of many such put in at various spots on the coast in an effort to generate electricity by wave action. For a short period the machine actually did produce enough electricity to illuminate the lights along the Strand. The trolley line which ran along the ocean from Playa del Rey to Redondo affected local lighting, too—the railway sold electricity to homes and businesses, and the Strand lights and those in homes along the right of way always dimmed when the streetcars came by.

From the beach you'll notice that the pier is supported by pairs of stout brown concrete pilings, their sandy-textured hides and soft lines suggesting surreal elephant's legs or a structure by Gaudi. The pilings were manufactured on the spot: each weighs twenty-four tons and is hollow, reinforced with twisted steel rods. They were jetted into place by a stream of water, and are sunk about ten feet in the sand.

Eager to attract out-of-towners, Manhattanites opened their new pier on July 5, 1920 with the works—parade, dance, band concert, and a drawing for a lot on Center Street, won by a man from Pasadena. Banners strung around town read "Welcome, Frolic, Happiness and Hail." Townfolk soon added a bath-house and a restaurant on the beach end of the pier, with a cafe underneath for bathers. But to ensure that only a "better class of people" would be attracted, they allowed no concessions on the beach, to "keep clear of the element that always comes with the cheap amusements."

From the pier you can see that a sand ridge three streets high faces the ocean; and accordingly, town property is either in the "sand" or the "soil" section. Early residents avoided the ocean front, preferring to live back of the shifting dunes and blowing sand, till the women of the town began to plant iceplant to hold the sand in place. Residents also formed the habit of carrying a hammer and nails on their strolls along the Boardwalk, to keep it in good repair.

In 1928 the pier was extended 200 feet beyond the pavilion, to provide moorings for yachts and a deep sea fishing barge. Storms in '40 and '41 destroyed the extension, returning the pier to its present proportions. After Pearl Harbor the pier was blacked out, and guarded by military personnel from possible sabotage. When submarine sightings were reported they also strung barbed wire along the beach, and patrolled it with dogs.

In downtown Manhattan Beach, adjacent to the pier, you'll find restaurants, boutiques and other shops, including the Candy Cottage halfway up the hill on the left, making pralines, turtles and elegant birthday treats at the same spot for thirty years; among the local amusements which are definitely not "cheap."

VENICE PIER

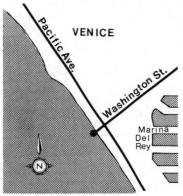

The shallow bowl of Santa Monica Bay holds six piers, and the ghosts of a dozen more, old Venice and Ocean Park the seaside playground of young Los Angeles, growing up with Southern California. New Venice Pier is as unlike the old as you could imagine: all of concrete, it hops across the sand into the sea on a single row of massive white pilings—no shadowy nooks here where evil might lurk. At intervals staggered outsets on slanting piles provide lateral support, and more rail space for fishermen. Smooth-floored, 16 x 1,310 feet, the pier is irresistible to skaters.

Shiny concrete—indestructible, yes? Well, sort of. During the storms of January and March 1983, the pier held up fine. Only, the roaring waves ate away

55

the beach till it undermined the bicycle path and the entering ramp of the pier, which in turn cracked from its own weight and collapsed in rubble. The intact pier sat there all summer, fenced off and unused, while the bureaucratic wheels groaned oh-so-slowly toward its repair. Now it's open again, and busier than ever.

The pier head is a 120-foot circle, centered by a bait-tackle-snack building where you can rent poles and get live bait. A solid wall encloses sides and end, making this pier unusually safe for the small children which abound, exploring strange bait buckets and poking other people's catches—Venice is a family fishing pier. But the wall also cuts off the natural ventilation of the sea breeze, and contains those bits of trash which usually fly away (yes, littering the beach downcoast). By the end of a long weekend, the pungency of ripe and overflowing trash cans blocks out the tang of the salt air.

Anyway, the fishermen don't seem to mind. The crowd mirrors L.A.'s ethnic and cultural mix—Indonesians in batik headbands, little kids in Princeton 19?? T-shirts, and inevitably the solitary teenager hauling his/her own environment along, a big transistor radio endlessly spinning a protective cocoon of sound.

To improve fishing, the Department of Fish and Game in 1966 created an artificial reef by dumping 4,000 tons of quarry rock around the end of the pier. The most common catches here are bonito, mackerel and jack smelt.

On Washington Street just up from the pier are bike and skate rentals and a tackle shop, boutiques, and food ranging from a fast falafel or taco to sit-down seafood, some of it served outside.

Just upcoast you'll see a rock groin put in to protect the beach, and a little beyond it the breakwater which sheltered the old Venice Pier, with beach sand accumulated behind it; and maybe some old pilings sticking up, uncovered in the last storm. They're all that remain of what Boardwalk historians call the real Venice Pier. Three miles upcoast lies Santa Monica Pier: the beach between is unbroken...the gaudy tumult of Venice and Ocean Park, the giant amusement piers with their noise, stink and dazzle, which made this stretch the Coney Island of the West for four decades, have vanished without a trace.

Old Venice Pier was only part of the dream of Abbot Kinney, who envisioned a community here where he could bring about an American Renaissance. He laid out nineteen miles of canals, and built covered arcades along Windward Avenue and an auditorium on the pier where Sarah Bernhardt played Camille in 1905, the summer it opened.

But Kinney found that the crowds wanted fun, not culture; and that's what they got. By the 1910s Venice was the finest amusement pier on the coast, with two roller coasters, ten-cent camel rides, Kid Ory's New Orleans style jazz in the dance hall—the works.

Ocean Park Pier, September 1926. Remains of the roller coaster destroyed in the 1924 fire lie alongside the rebuilt pier. Venice Pier, visible in the background, also had two roller coasters, one of them parallel to the breakwater.

And the area was a natural for making the newest magic, moving pictures. In late 1907, two men who had shot the first half of their one-reel (twelve-minute) film, *The Count of Monte Cristo,* in Chicago fled the midwestern winter and came to California to finish it. Somewhere along here they filmed the climactic scene where Edmond escapes from his island prison—using a different actor, as it happened (but who would notice?). Hollywood's film industry was born.

The piers provided ready-made sets for such early movie makers as Mack Sennett. His 1914 comedy, *Tillie's Punctured Romance*, reached its climax on the end of Venice Pier, with Marie Dressler being pulled in and out of the water like a yo-yo by the Keystone Kops, while Charlie Chaplin swooned nearby.

Another attraction: as neighboring towns voted themselves dry, Venice became one of the few places left where you could legally get a drink. . . until Prohibition arrived for all Californians in July 1919.

The growing popularity of the automobile probably contributed most to Venice's decline. No major thoroughfare passed close by, and the area lacked parking: at the same time the streetcars, which for decades had carried the crowds to the beaches, were slowed by the growing traffic, became less competitive and eventually died.

In 1947 Los Angeles refused to renew its lease on the tidelands, and ordered the pier demolished. When I saw it in the late '40s, all that remained was the wide wooden ramp, a few boarded-up booths, and the blackened framework of the Big Dipper thrusting up from the sand like the ribs of some extinct sea creature. Today Venice is undergoing a kind of renaissance; but looking upcoast from the new Venice Pier, the only sign of the old is that fragment of Abbot Kinney's granite breakwater, trailing a few streamers of foam onshore.

Here at the new Venice Pier there are plenty of quieter pleasures—volleyball nets on the sand just south of the pier in front of the parking lot, a stand renting bikes and rollerskates. Fat palm trees flank the foot of the pier, fronds rattling in the wind; skaters and bikers and boats on the water—everything is moving. The nineteen-mile bike trail along Santa Monica Bay turns inland here at Washington to go around Marina del Rey. You can bike one way and take a free shuttle bus back.

The jetty and breakwater you see to the south protect the mouth of the marina, and sailboats and power boats come spilling out when the weather's good. The detached section of breakwater parallel with the shore had to be added after the marina was built, when it was discovered that the original design didn't keep breakers from forming and rolling into the mouth of the marina. . . . And a whale-shaped sign on the lifeguard tower says, "Please, no dogs, horses, fires or alcohol." That's Bigtown; always looking out for us.

SANTA MONICA PIER

Santa Monica Pier with roller coaster and La Monica Ballroom, seen from the Palisades in the 1920s; before the building of the breakwater—note the narrow beach.

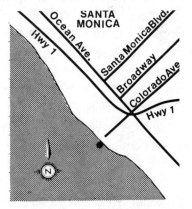

Santa Monica has been the quintessential pier, having managed through the years to distill all the elements into a mellow and unmistakeable "pierness." Starting down the steep incline from Colorado, you get the whole thing—the big red and yellow merry-go-round building with its funky towers, and the shops strung up the pier, sand and sea and sky spread out, and....

Nothing quite compares with that sudden empty feeling in your stomach when a familiar place is just—gone. The inland half of the pier is still there and almost the same, fish market, video arcade, the curio place and part of the big parking lot. But the double-deck end with the harbormaster's office above the Port Cafe on the lower level, winches, boat rental, sport-fishing office—the whole outer half was obliterated by a few swipes of Mother Ocean.

True, it's happened before—in fact, the very first pier built here was demolished, not by nature but by its owners, in their efforts to dominate Southern California shipping.

In January 1983, during a stormy season which brought the area three times its normal rainfall, Santa Monica like many other coastal piers was badly damaged. A month later, another storm combined with high tides again hit the pier: eighteen-foot waves rolling over it washed away three cars and scuttled a large truck and two cranes which had already been put to work clearing up earlier damage. Tons of wreckage piled up on the sand.

Hardly a trace remains now of the breakwater off the end of the pier. It was originally surfaced, with a suspension bridge extending to it from the end of the pier so that you could walk out to the boats moored along its inner edge. The breakwater's presence slowed the current and created the wide beach just north of the pier, where there's almost no surf.

The two-story building housing the carousel had seven apartments built upstairs, overlooking the leaping horses which have been beautifully restored: most are unoccupied now. Opened in 1914, the carousel was recently designated a museum, but you can still ride the big carved wooden beauties on Saturdays and Sundays for twenty-five cents, soaring to the organ music while fragments of watchers and coastline turn past in the central mirrors. If the setting is more than usually familiar, maybe you've seen it in a movie—*The Sting* or *Ride a Pink Horse* to name two.

A sign on the outside of the carousel building thanks "the people of Santa Monica" for saving both building and pier after the city council in 1973 voted unanimously to tear it down because some of the outer pilings were rotted. This pier has had more than one struggle with conflicting interests.

In the beginning, the Shoo-Fly Landing built here in the early 1870s was used to ship *brea* (tar) hauled by oxen from Colonel Hancock's Brea Ranch and loaded onto steamers, which carried it to San Francisco to pave that great city's streets. In 1875 the Los Angeles & Independence Railway replaced it with a 1,700-foot wharf and depot out on the end, and coastal steamers began to stop regularly, passengers and goods being carried on into Los Angeles by train.

The railway built a pavilion on the beach with bowling alley, billiard room and roller-skating rink, and Santa Monicans looked forward to increasing trade and prosperity, since passengers arriving from the north were twelve hours closer to Los Angeles than if they went on down to San Pedro. But in 1877 the Los Angeles & Independence sold out to Southern Pacific, which in 1878 raised freight rates and moved the depot inland to encourage the use of its facilities in San Pedro.

Next the railroad sent out a team of engineers, who inspected the pier and declared that it was badly damaged by teredos (marine boring worms), and so unsafe for trains. Company officials declared repairs too expensive and ordered the pier demolished, over the protests of townspeople, who rightly believed their budding town would suffer. When workers tried to pull out the redwood pilings, they couldn't be budged: the men were reduced to chopping them off one by one, and the pilings were discovered to be almost intact.

But Santa Monica hadn't seen the last of the railway piers. Growing Los Angeles lacked an adequate seaport, and Santa Monica craved the riches such a development would bring, as did Redondo and San Pedro/Wilmington. A Congressional survey recommended San Pedro as the site for the harbor; but Collis Huntington, whose Southern Pacific Railway now held a monopoly in the Santa Monica area, determined that this would be Port Los Angeles. And so in 1890 he began building California's longest pier, then or since.

Based just north of Santa Monica Canyon, the Long Wharf extended 4,720 feet out into water thirty to fifty feet deep. Its outer end was 130 feet wide and canted toward Point Dume to hold seven spurs on the outer end; a fresh water system, boathouse and fishing landing part way out, warehouse, depot with a public restaurant, and a big coal bunker.

First ship to dock at the Long Wharf was the collier *San Mateo*, in May 1893. Between then and 1896, 759 ships called at Port Los Angeles, 52 sailing vessels and 707 steam-powered. But the San Pedro site was favored by many interests who feared Huntington's monopoly, among them the Los Angeles Chamber of Commerce. After a long struggle, in which Huntington exerted all his influence, work on the San Pedro breakwater finally began: Santa Monica had lost out. (Some of us think she actually won.)

For years the Long Wharf was a popular destination for sightseers, and the Pacific Electric Railway regularly ran excursionists out for "an ocean voyage on wheels"; but in 1908 the Pacific Coast Steamships stopped calling, and in 1910 all regular shipping there came to an end. Neglected, its remains were soon destroyed by the sea. Today the only visible reminder of the Long Wharf is the tunnel under Ocean Avenue and Colorado that connects the Santa Monica Freeway with Coast Highway: it was dug for the railway line which ran out to Port Los Angeles.

Another pier was built here at the foot of Colorado in 1912, and Santa Monicans finally had their municipal pier. When adjoining Looff Pier with its carousel and Blue Streak Racing Coaster opened in 1916, the inlanders started coming...La Monica Ballroom opened in July 1924 to a first-day crowd of 50,000. Advertised as the largest ballroom in the world, La Monica had room enough for 5,000 dancers and 5,000 more spectators, and it became a coastal landmark with its vaguely Byzantine towers all outlined in lights glittering across the water on summer nights.

During the '20s another, more wicked brand of entertainment moved into the bay, and the customers lined up for water taxis which carried them out to the

gambling ships, *Texas, Tango, Showboat, Rex*, anchored offshore. Even after Prohibition ended, the floating casinos continued to be popular with gambling Californians.

Staying more than three miles offshore, the ships were thus on the high seas and outside state jurisdiction, and returned a handsome profit to their operators. There were hazards: in 1935 the *Monte Carlo* was raided by eleven "pirates" who robbed employees and customers of $40,000 in money and jewels. Like something from one of Raymond Chandler's stories...poet of L.A.'s darker side, Chandler used the piers and gambling ships as settings in several of his 1930s mystery novels and short stories.

Most notorious gambling ship was Tony Cornero's *Rex*, which began life in 1887 as the steel-hulled, four-masted barkentine *Kenilworth* and had served in the Alaskan salmon cannery trade. Cornero knew this coast well, having run in cargoes of Scotch during Prohibition and reportedly beaching them in Malibu and elsewhere before he was temporarily jailed in '29.

Cornero's *Rex* offered a faro bank, blackjack, stud poker, horse race betting, tango (bingo), chuck-a-luck, bird cage, Chinese lottery or high spade, 150 slot machines and 11 roulette wheels. Running twenty-four hours a day, it served (or skinned) a maximum of 1,900 squirrels at a time, as Cornero called his customers, cleared $100,000 a month for Cornero, and supremely frustrated California law enforcement officials, among them the state attorney general (and later Supreme Court chief justice) Earl Warren.

In July 1939, their day came: the four gambling ships were boarded by a force of 250 ax-swinging deputies—that is, the other three were. Cornero's crew stood off the boarders with a heavy landing net and high-pressure water hoses. Four months later the State Supreme Court declared that Santa Monica, from points Dume to Vicente, was in fact a bay and not open ocean. The *Rex* was finished...but not Cornero, who gave it one more try, in Long Beach of all places.

Pier-goers today lean more to outdoor recreations, fishing and roller-skating, biking—there's a bicycle trail separate from the Boardwalk, starting north of here at California Street and running south 19.1 miles, almost all along the shore, ending beyond Redondo. And famous Muscle Beach, just south of the pier, usually has some spectacularly built devotees working out on the bars and the travelling rings.

But, unlike the other coastal piers, Santa Monica hasn't been rebuilt yet. It's a drowsy place, with only one open seafood restaurant, a few fishermen leaning on the railing, a bag lady sleeping undisturbed on one of the neat blue-and-white benches. The high-rollers are gone, the excitement is past. Will Santa Monica rise again?

MALIBU PIER

Malibu Pier, at the northern edge of Santa Monica Bay, is a narrow wooden pier, pleasantly rustic, painted the traditional blue and white. The State bought the pier in 1980 and a leisurely refurbishing had been under way, until the '83 storms drastically rearranged the schedule. Now it's open again, the half-day boat *Lenbrooke* idling at the landing out on the end as it takes on passengers morning and afternoon—from September to May the all-day boat, *Aquarius*, goes out, too, fishing rock cod.

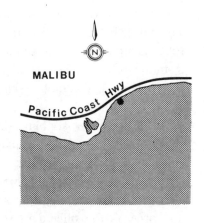

Out on the end of the pier a pair of two-story Cape Cod-style buildings face one another, the right-hand with a widow's walk around its upper story. This building has been unused for several years, but the one on the left holds a snack shop and tackle stand where you can get live bait any day, starting at 6:00 A.M.

Alice's Restaurant at the foot of the pier has a glassed-in view of Malibu's most famous public feature, Surfriders' Beach. Long breakers roll in along Malibu Point with a broad public beach, memorialized by a gaggle of *Gidget* movies. Surfers describe it as "one of the most perfect summer breaks in all of California," the waves here exhibiting "the best form on the whole Pacific Coast." Sadly, they're surrounded by summer crowds, traffic jams and nonexistent parking.

From the pier you see the hills rising behind the highway, and the bay curving away southward. On maps of the coast this cove is still labelled Keller's Shelter, after its first American owner, Mathew Keller. The land was all part of the vast Rancho Topanga Malibu Sequit, named for three Indian villages in the area. Keller bought it in 1860 and raised cattle, planted vineyards, and helped develop California wines. Upon his death, "the Malibu" was bought in 1891 by Frederick Rindge, coincidentally a descendant of New England Puritans and a teetotaler.

Rindge eventually owned twenty-four miles of coastline, from Las Flores Canyon northward, and a 400-foot pier was built at this same spot by the Rindge family around 1940. When Rindge died in 1905, his widow, May, determined to keep the property intact. She spent the next thirty years fighting to keep homesteaders out and railways and highways from being built across her property, using high fences and armed guards, and finally dynamiting her own roads. The only coastal route between Ventura and Santa Monica lay along this beach at low tide: the State of California wanted to build the Coast Highway, and the battle went all the way to the Supreme Court, where May Rindge lost.

In 1917 the first piece of Malibu beachfront property was leased, and John Gilbert, Barbara Stanwyck, Ronald Colman and Dolores Del Rio soon became part of the first wave which settled the Malibu Colony just upcoast.

The Rindge Pier was partly washed away by storms and the remainder torn down in 1943 when William Huber bought this 650-foot section of oceanfront. He built the present 700-foot pier and the pair of wood-paneled buildings, and opened the pier according to ancient tradition, on the Fourth of July in 1945. His son sold the pier and the adjoining beach-front property to the state in 1980 for $2.5million, frontage then being valued at $10,000 a front foot.

Alongside the railing, a reminder of Malibu's continuing show biz connections: two young men in turtlenecks were having an animated discussion in some completely unfamiliar language, of which we could understand only "CBS" and "piloti."

HUENEME PIER

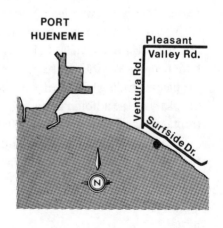

PORT HUENEME

Pleasant Valley Rd.

Ventura Rd.

Surfside Dr.

N

Hueneme Pier is not only hard to pro-nounce (it's Wy-NEE-me), it's well off the beaten track, a quiet small-town spot used mostly by local fishermen. Of unfinished wood weathered to a warm brown and with no buildings on it, the pier is a peculiar shape. It starts out straight for about 400 feet, turns left for maybe 50 feet, and then right-angles again across the shore and over the water, ending in a wide T platform.

From here to Point Concepcion the coast lies almost due east and west. The coastal plain back of Hueneme extends inland ten or twelve miles till it reaches the lower ranges and spurs of the Santa Ynez range trailing away, and southward the higher Santa Monicas start, with 3,000-foot Old Boney sticking up dark and rugged, all of it enhancing the feeling of solitude.

Downcoast between here and Point Mugu is a power plant with the traditional red-and-white-striped smokestacks. The three-mile stretch of uncrowded beach has several good surfing spots. Directly in line with the end of the pier lies big Santa Cruz Island—it and its fellows, San Miguel, Santa Rosa and Anacapa, protect the Santa Barbara Channel and this shoreline by partially deflecting stormy seas.

Behind the pier clusters of new condominiums line the ocean front, and a sidewalk curves along the beach for a mile or so in each direction. Two parking areas on the downcoast side are surrounded by clusters of young palms and rosemary groundcover spreading thick and glossy, thriving in the salt air. Beyond, the beach is open and mostly undisturbed, gently mounded with patches of natural vegetation.

On either side of the pier on the beach are several concrete pads, each divided by central walls into four sections containing table and benches, some with barbeques alongside; and there are climbing bars for children on the sand.

also armed. Barnard came over: he and Bard had words. Barnard broke the top fence rail and stepped inside: Bard grappled with him, and threw him back out. The fence-building went on, as the settlers—squatters?—maintained a picket line around it at a distance. Some of them built a scaffold, and threw a rope over it with a noose tied in its end.

By nightfall Bard and his men finished fencing themselves in, and they spent the night on the beach without a fire, to avoid making possible targets of themselves. Next morning Bard and Barnard met again; but instead of a row, they reached an agreement. Both sides agreed that whoever won the land case would sell the disputed lands to the other at a fair price, and the squatters were to be paid for the value of any improvements they'd made. In the meantime, building of the wharf was to go on unhampered, since it was clearly a benefit to all concerned.

Hueneme Wharf opened two months later, the first major wharf between Santa Cruz and San Pedro. Bard won the boundary dispute, and most of the settlers bought their land. But a few of them moved on—among them "Old Man" Clanton and his boys, who went to Arizona Territory, where they got mixed up with cattle rustling and the Earp brothers and came to a bad end.

The 900-foot wharf ran into eighteen-foot water, and was forty feet across the end. Soon it was extended to 1,426 feet, where the water was twenty-two feet deep

The cement-block tackle stand/snack shop at the foot of the pier dispenses the usual hamburgers and frozen bait, and rents fishing poles and two-seated tricycles. There are four video games here now, and a handwritten sign: *No loud noise or vulgar language.* The new restroom building alongside is also of cement brick, with angled walls and stainless steel fixtures.

You can see right away that these are regular fishermen—one woman hauls her gear out in the basket of her yellow tricycle with everything in its appointed spot, and an older couple together pull a loaded red wagon. Plenty of kids learning how: here a boy brings in a perch, his father rattling instructions at him in Spanish as he swings it over the rail and the other kids come running to take a look.

Hueneme hasn't always been so peaceful. The first pier on this section of the coast was built in 1871, but only after an armed nose-to-nose confrontation. The land was part of La Colonia, a Spanish grant to which Thomas Bard held claim; but the boundaries of La Colonia weren't clearly established, and several families had settled at this spot, believing it to be public domain. When Bard wanted to build a wharf, his attorney advised him to fence off the three landward sides of the site to establish "constructive possession."

Before dawn on a May morning in 1871, Bard and four other armed men appeared at the site and began building a flimsy fence. About sixty members of the local Settlers League gathered nearby at Barnard's General Store, some of them at low tide, and corrals were built on the wharf to hold cattle and sheep being shipped out.

In October 1877, when the new Ventura Wharf went down in a storm, Hueneme stood unharmed. Ventura was again destroyed by high waves in January 1878, while the wharf at Hueneme only tilted over somewhat and had to be righted. Said the *Ventura Free Press*, "The wharf at Wynema is the only one between San Francisco and Santa Monica which stood the storm unless it be the small one at Gaviota....This is creditable to the skills of the builders, Messrs. Salisbury and Frazier, who also built the pier at Santa Monica." Maybe so; but Mr. Salisbury built Ventura's unlucky wharf, too.

Hueneme became a busy port, in 1887 shipping almost 400,000 sacks of barley, 7,000 hogs, and wheat, corn, potatoes and other produce, including honey and mustard-seed, all hauled out to the ships by horses pulling flatcars along a track. During threshing season, long lines of teams waited to unload at the two big warehouses at the foot of the wharf.

In the coastal trade there were still many two-masted sailing schooners, or windjammers; but in the '70s and '80s a hybrid developed—a steam schooner, with a box-like cabin on the after-deck, and a smokestack: it burned coal. Like most coastal piers, Hueneme was subject to sudden storms. The steamer *Bonita* was loading when waves came up, and she had to cut her lines to get away. The *Yaquina* went aground on a sandbar in heavy fog and was pounded by heavy seas. Her hull lay near the pier for years, till it finally disintegrated.

The railroad came through in 1898, putting an end to shipping here. Worse, the train bypassed Hueneme for nearby Oxnard, which was growing up around a sugar beet factory, and Hueneme dwindled into a quiet little village. You can find traces of the older town a couple of blocks inland, around Market and Pomona, where the local historical society is housed in a 1925 bank building under a big tree.

The town's name was originally a Chumash Indian word meaning *half-way* or *resting place*, probably given as they traveled between Mugu and Ventura. It was variously spelled Y-nee-ma and Wyneema. Oldtimers still say "Way-nay-ma," and the official spelling was Wynema until 1940, when the Post Office changed it.

In 1940 a 300-acre harbor was created here, and in 1942 the federal government bought it and expanded it into the "Home of the Pacific Seabees." Upcoast two blocks, you can see the masts and cranes in Port Hueneme Harbor thrusting above the rooftops. During World War II a good part of the supplies for Pacific armed forces was shipped from Hueneme, the only deep-water port between Los Angeles and San Francisco.

Today the old cruisers are tied up and rusting, and freighters and commercial fishing boats use the harbor. We saw the Exxon ships *High Tide* and *Alberta Tide* from New Orleans tied up, and the three big yellow booms of the Japanese freighter *Tama Rex* were loading pallets of Arizona grapefruit.

Hueneme's original wharf lasted till '39. In 1956 an outfall sewer was built with a pier over it which residents used for fishing, until the Army engineers began their bi-annual pumping of sand from the Channel Islands Harbor in Oxnard. The sand widened the beach so much that the pier no longer reached the water. Residents got up a petition for a new fishing pier, and the present 1,400-foot pier, built in 1968, is the result.

Its broad surrounding beach, courtesy of the Army Corps of Engineers, is periodically eroded away by the sea, which explains that funny jog in the pier's stem: it follows a buried seawall. Local observers say that during recent winter storms the beach was eaten away to within several feet of the paving. Said one, "You could've used those cement pads out there for diving platforms."

VENTURA PIER

Ventura Pier juts out from its bluff below the freeway like a giant hockey stick. The coast faces south here and so does the 1,700-foot pier, except for its broad outer end, which jogs southwest—the better to meet storm waves running down the Santa Barbara Channel. Last rebuilt in 1928 (and repaired several times since), its shape is a reminder that it, too, was once a working wharf.

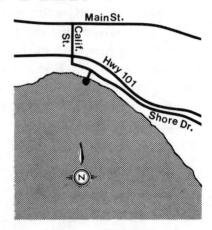

Harbor Drive passes just behind the foot of the pier, where there's a small unloading area for a passenger unable to climb stairs. Otherwise you park below at beach level on either side of the pier, and climb up the stairs on the upcoast side. The Pier Fish House, slate blue walls with white

The bow of the steamship *Coos Bay* was driven into Ventura Pier during a storm in December 1914. The wooden ship was shortly thereafter driven right through the pier, wrecking it. The hull lay to the east of the pier for several years.

trim and a sort of wainscot of blond varnished wood along the bottom, sits squarely on the foot of the pier—from a window table you can look along the length of the pier. And a new wedge-shaped outside dining area with glass walls points down the pier, with water views in both directions.

Farther out are a tackle-bait-snack shop (no live bait available), and a restroom building. The pier deck, of two-by-six boards set about two inches apart, is not the place for high heels, except on the solid six-foot walkway down the middle.

All along the pier's east side runs a low wooden box about a foot square, very handy to sit on and for cutting bait. This long box originally held the wiring for the pier's electric lights, attached to the back of it, said a city worker: but the state engineering report declares that it was built to accommodate an oil pipeline which was never installed.

Cut into the deck on the outer end of the pier are two small fishing wells. And there are fish at Ventura: one morning we watched a man bring in a big halibut.

From out here, the landward view is distinctive, too—the city is only six blocks deep at this point, backed by a row of low golden hills which are treeless and mostly unbuilt-on. "And they'll stay that way," said Judie Kesson, assistant to Ventura's city manager. "It's definitely city planning policy." If you look just to the right of the beachfront Holiday Inn, you'll see the stately white City Hall sitting enthroned at the top of California Street, framed by the hills.

The city is still officially San Buenaventura, named after its mission. When the Southern Pacific Railroad line reached the town in 1887 the name was shortened to Ventura on its timetables, and eventually the post office began to use this form.

Early pictures of Ventura wharf show it with the same dog-leg on its outer end, and railroad tracks along its length. The first wharf was built in 1872 by the same Mr. Salisbury who was busy lengthening Stearns Wharf in Santa Barbara. Ventura Wharf was originally 1,200 feet long, extending into twenty-four-foot water to serve larger vessels.

A peculiarity: the wharf was built angling downward, dropping twelve inches every 100 feet, so that it was twelve feet lower on its outer end, imitating by half the drop in the ocean floor—which seems exactly the wrong slant. Modern piers are built with a rise: the deeper the water, the higher the potential wave, since a wave's height can reach seventy to seventy-five percent of the water's depth at a particular point without breaking.

The pier flourished for a time—in fact, in June 1878, the redwood pilings were reported to be green with new shoots; but it went out in a storm that December, and several times thereafter.

In the 1913-14 flood, the Ventura River, which empties into the ocean west of the pier, brought down an enormous amount of material, widening the beach by about 400 feet and creating sand shoals that made docking difficult. On December 14, 1915, the small coastal steamer *Coos Bay* was tied up to the pier when she was caught in a rising swell.

Her captain evidently was anxious to get her out into the open sea, having had trouble at this same spot earlier...in 1911 she had broken loose, empty, and drifted onto the beach. As the captain swung the ship around in his haste to get away, her stern struck bottom and then crashed into the wharf—in fact, she was driven right through it by the heavy seas, making a sizable gap. The ship grounded permanently in shallow water just east of the pier and parallel with it. The hulk stayed there for years, till it was beached further east by a storm in '48.

Damage done by the *Coos Bay* was finally repaired in 1917, and the pier was extended 500 feet. In 1926 another big storm came in, destroying the pier and drowning the wharf company's bookkeeper, who went down in the wreckage. His body was never recovered.

Once again the pier was rebuilt, since considerable shipping was still moving through Ventura, mostly lumber coming in and petroleum products being loaded into tank steamers. Fire destroyed the landward section in 1935, and the next reconstruction included a four-foot-gauge railway track along the west side to haul freight, the cars being moved by tractor.

The last cargo of lumber was unloaded here in 1940. You can still see two iron bollards or tie-downs, relics of Ventura's shipping days. The city turned the pier over to the state in 1948, and it's now part of a state park.

A bright, chilly afternoon: all the fishermen are lined up along the east rail, their backs hunched against the wind. A Standard Oil work barge is anchored off the end of the pier, with a few seagulls hanging around it. Downcoast, rows of eucalyptus windbreakers bending...Point Mugu partly protects the pier from storms driving up the coast. Straight inland, a tall red and white antenna stands up on the hilltop.

The end of the pier is fenced off, having been damaged once again by the storms of '83, and the end railing is gone: it'll be repaired when the city locates some funding. The pier sways a little in the surge, but we're almost too far from shore to hear the surf. People stroll out, hair flying, to see what they're catching...not much, a few kingfish; but that doesn't seem to matter. Two city workers with sledgehammers ramble along, stopping every so often to wham the deck. They're looking to drive in any spikes that have worked loose...pier-keeping is never done.

STEARNS WHARF

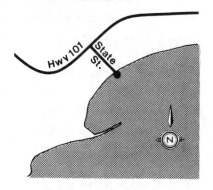

Out on the end of Santa Barbara's Stearns Wharf at 10:00 A.M. on a crystal morning, fishermen (mostly kids—it's summertime) pulling in smallish mackerel one after another and two pelicans paddling around, staying within range of the cleaning sink—trying to take it all in, get to the essence of its charm.

The dramatic view, yes, that's part of it; dark tree-covered slopes and hills and the red roofs of this favored city, and rising behind everything the protective mountain wall of the Santa Ynez, colors and textures shifting in the changing light. And here you are, at center stage.

To the west the yacht harbor is packed with masts crowded behind the curving arm of the breakwater, and all along the ocean front stand the tall old palm trees. Around the broad end of the pier there are boats moored and you can see them clearly, the pier has no railings out here. This pier is short-legged.

Shut down in 1975 after the old Harbor Restaurant burned (a beautiful place, made from an old ship with its shaped timbers and carvings), for several years the pier lay across the harbor like the skeleton of a stranded sea-beast, visited only by the gulls. Rebuilt and reopened, it's once again a focus of city life and you can drive out onto it, with the loose planks making that familiar rumbling under your wheels.

At intervals along the pier there are framed descriptions of local sea life, animals and fishes and birds from the Museum of Natural History. In the cluster of shops to the left you can buy candy, clothes, shells and curios, have your palm read, taste wine, visit a gallery with work by local artists; and there's a fast-food place with benches outside overlooking the water. The fish market has live crabs and lobster, clams or oysters on the half-shell—on a Saturday afternoon, people were queued up around the corner of the building.

The new Harbor Restaurant has a glassed-in deck upstairs, with a view that's even more panoramic. Alongside, the seventy-foot flagpole is a pine mast made in 1901 for the Hereschoff schooner *Cock Robin*.

Ironically, the new pier was born from disaster. Funds won from the oil companies for damages in the 1969 oil spill were used to restore the wharf, so that its commercial activities need only pay for its maintenance. The city's "over-the-water plank park" cost $5 million to restore, a sum which would have astounded its originator, that one-legged Vermonter, Abel Stearns.

When Stearns decided in 1876 to build a wharf long enough to handle ocean-going vessels, the town was making do with a short wharf at the end of Chapala Street, built four years earlier and reaching only to the kelp line. Passengers and goods still had to be brought through the breakers in surfboats, or lighters, and carried ashore piggyback by strong sailors. They were expected to tip the sailor first: those who didn't risked an "accidental" bath.

Stearns ran his 1,500-foot wharf out into forty-foot water, so that coastal ships could tie up to it in good weather—this is an open roadstead, and no breakwater existed then. The wharf began a new era for the little mission town, connecting it with the outside world. However, Stearns' wharfage fees were only half the cost of lightering, and local businessmen retaliated by getting the city to charge Stearns a fifty-dollar license fee, which he refused to pay.

During a severe storm in January 1878, a barge broke loose and smashed into the little Chapala Street wharf, demolishing it. About this time the steamer *Senator* arrived, but, seeing the weather too rough to unload freight or passengers, went on to San Pedro. Later that night a Chinese junk in the harbor dragged her anchors and crashed into the short pier too. The mass of wreckage drifted east, hit Stearns Wharf midway, and tore out a hundred feet of it. Over the next several days another thousand feet of the pier were smashed, and freight waiting in the warehouse out on the end had to be lightered back to shore.

Stearns refused to rebuild his wharf until the fifty-dollar fee was rescinded, and freight and passengers began to bypass the town, although the three lighters, the *Baptist Dugout*, the *Blatherskite* and the *Spiritual Alliance,* temporarily did a good ship-to-shore business, charging passengers fifty cents apiece. Townspeople, seeing business passing them by, made the city council rescind the fee, and Stearns rebuilt his wharf.

In 1880 Stearns built another 1,450-foot Y wharf curving out from between

Anacapa and Santa Barbara streets and join his first wharf midway. It carried a railroad spur so that lumber could be unloaded quickly: but the Y was difficult to maintain, and broke up after a decade. Numerous other piers were built along this shoreline—a 1908 map shows sixteen of them in the vicinity.

Santa Barbara's mild climate and healthful springs made the city a resort where wealthy easterners came for the winter. The completion of Southern Pacific's coast line in 1901 spelled the end of passenger travel by steamship, but freight hauling continued for some time: in fact, the wharf's largest lumber shipment ever was landed in January 1922. The wharf had almost been destroyed in October 1921, when the 600-room Potter Hotel burned down in a fifty-mile-per-hour santana (offshore wind). Flying embers set fire to the palm fronds along the ocean front, and kindled a number of fires on the wharf. Stearns' original wharf finally had to be replaced by the city in 1928.

In the '30s a new business enterprise was added when the gambling ship *Miss Hollywood* anchored offshore outside the three-mile limit and U.S. jurisdiction, her customers boarding water taxis at the wharf. When Pearl Harbor was attacked in December 1941, the Coast Guard took over the pier for the duration of the war. From 1945 to 1947, the wharf was owned briefly by a group which included James Cagney and his brothers.

In 1925, Max Fleischman and the city began to build the breakwater which gave Santa Barbara its long-dreamed-of harbor, now sheltering about 800 commercial and pleasure craft. Between 1873 and 1921 the Army Corps of Engineers had made five reports on such a project, all of them somewhat unfavorable, citing the strong eastward-flowing current which carries sand washed into the ocean all along the forty-five mile stretch of coast from Point Concepcion, depositing this sand along the beaches.

When the 1,500-foot L-shaped breakwater was built, sand immediately began to build up around it, depositing at a rate of 775 cubic yards a day. At the same time the beaches downcoast, no longer fed by this sand, became seriously eroded. To correct the problem the Army engineers pumped out and redistributed 600,000 cubic yards of sand, but the harbor has to be re-dredged every two or three years. Today the growing sand shoal filling the harbor and moving shoreward is clearly visible from the pier.

Over on the harbor's waterfront are restaurants, shops and two piers, and you can rent motorboats, sailboats, sailboards, and rowboats. The half-mile break-water has been surfaced with a walkway and protected by a cement wall: you can walk out to the end with the spray from the open ocean coming over sometimes, and admire reborn Stearns Wharf. And on the wharf itself, the fishermen, the weather and the birds are doing their best to tone down that glossy new look.

GOLETA PIER

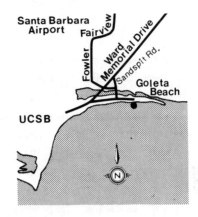

Goleta Pier points straight at the Channel Islands, Santa Cruz in particular, which may explain why this stretch of water is so calm. In December and in July we've seen canoes and catamarans launched easily through the surf, and a boating class in progress beyond the breakers, with five kayaks and two canoes patiently paddling in circles.

The buildings on the point just upcoast are the University of California, Santa Barbara. From the university entrance you get a panoramic view of the coast and the islands, if it's clear enough, the pier and the surfers riding the long breakers beside Isla Vista Point. There's also some surfing downcoast.

It's a peaceful spot, semi-rural. Behind the pier Atascadero Creek empties into Goleta Slough and the stream flows parallel with the shoreline, emptying into the ocean just to the south—the beach is in fact a sandbar. A flock of ducks hanging around the parking lot spots the latest visitors and bustles over to beg, waddling after them and quacking loudly.

The narrow wooden pier was recently lengthened by 800 feet, making it 1,450 feet now. The day we were there, fishermen on the pier had caught several perch and a shovel-nose shark, and one man was catching anchovies.

The boat launch on the pier is available seven days a week—bring your own sling. You can also go sportfishing on the sixty-five-foot *Island Fox*, which makes alternate full-day and three-quarter-day trips. They go after bottom fish, since at last report they had no live bait available. The boat is refueled from a big yellow sphere which is towed out onto the pier.

You can also rent a boat, either powered or a Hobie cat, or get sailing instructions. Behind the beach a stretch of tree-shaded lawn has six or eight picnic tables with barbeques, and the six volleyball courts laid out on the sand get plenty of use. The Goleta Pier Galley has outside tables with umbrellas, and is open every day in summer. The new restaurant alongside seats over 100, and the plan is to have live music on weekends. And in the tackle shop the old familiar rhyme was hanging:

Early to bed
Early to rise
Fish like Hell
And make up lies.

Santa Barbara Municipal Airport is just behind the park, hidden by trees: it serves mostly small planes, but occasionally a large passenger plane takes off, shattering the cove's peaceful atmosphere.

The airport land was once part of Goleta Slough, mostly filled in now. Goleta Slough and Estuary were a deep-water port until the great floods of 1860-61, when Atascadero Creek deposited up to fourteen feet of silt over the whole area. In 1891 workers found a ten-foot anchor in the mud flats half a mile inland. It was made of laminated iron, of the type used in sixteenth-century caravels. A local history buff believes it was left there by Sir Francis Drake's expedition, and this is actually the site of "Drake's Bay"; other historians disagree.

This spot evidently was named Goleta, the Spanish word for schooner, after an American schooner that had been beached in the estuary by a high tide and was left there to rot.

A shore-whaling station operated here for a few years in the 1880s, closing down in 1890. The whales were towed ashore and rendered in seventy-gallon kettles, straight-sided (the better to fit in the ship's hold), heated over driftwood fires. And during the 1890s, the asphalt deposits under the UCSB site were mined for eight years, turning out sixty tons of asphaltum a day, some of which went to pave the streets of San Francisco and New Orleans' Vieux Carré. Goleta farmers were paid seventy-five cents a ton to haul the tar to the railroad wharf.

Goleta was once the largest city in California—in 1542, when Juan Cabrillo discovered the spot. More than a thousand Canalino Indians lived on Mescalitán Island, now covered by the road to UCSB, and there were six more Indian rancherias along the shores of the slough.

An old story had it that Cabrillo was buried in Goleta's cove. It's known that he broke his shoulder on San Miguel Island; gangrene set in and he died in January 1543, and was presumably buried there. But a tale handed down to the last Indians in the area described a coffined man in armor who was carried ashore here. . . .

GAVIOTA PIER

Northernmost of the Santa Barbara Channel piers is little Gaviota, and you have to know it's there to find it: you can see neither pier nor campground from the highway. Lying at the mouth of Gaviota Creek just where Highway 101 turns inland, the spot is dwarfed by the high railway trestle which bridges the gap in the bluffs.

Here the coastline is straight, with cliffs of creamy gold shale in both directions. Anchored to the upcoast cliff, the wooden

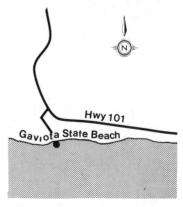

pier has an electric hoist for trailered boats, two dollars for one day, in and out. At the General Store, run by Bob and Nita Parker, were a multitude of pictures of halibut, and one of a calico bass. The store rents poles, and sells tackle and supplies.

"I try to think of what you might forget when you go camping, and stock it," Parker said. There are fifty-nine campsites in this state campground, and the pier fishermen are mostly campers.

Big patches of beer-brown kelp lift in the surge and wave around the pilings, an underground forest. "They get white sea bass out there," a fishermen said. On the pier they were bringing in perch and rock cod. "Sometimes you pick up a halibut here," he added, "but it's a problem to bring it up," pointing to the stringers of kelp.

Surfers also launch boats here, traveling by water to good surfing spots farther up which are inaccessible by land. Several drilling platforms are visible in both directions, and two passing tankers are silhouetted against the Channel Islands.

Gaviota Pass got its name in 1769 when one of Portola's soldiers shot a *gaviota*, a seagull. Coves in this area were used in the early 1800s by Yankee traders smuggling their goods in to the Californios, both anxious to avoid paying high Spanish tariffs. In the late 1800s old Gaviota Landing was built at this site, and handled produce from the Santa Ynez, Santa Rita and Las Cruces valleys, and wool and hides from the San Julian Ranch. In 1912 a storm destroyed that wharf.

The 2,756-acre park spreads inland a few miles, with trails entering it here and at Las Cruces. The beachside campground quite often fills up, said Park Aide Larry Ley. "Mostly people from inland, Santa Ynez, Lompoc," he said. "Not your regular city folks—a little more lusty. We get along fine."

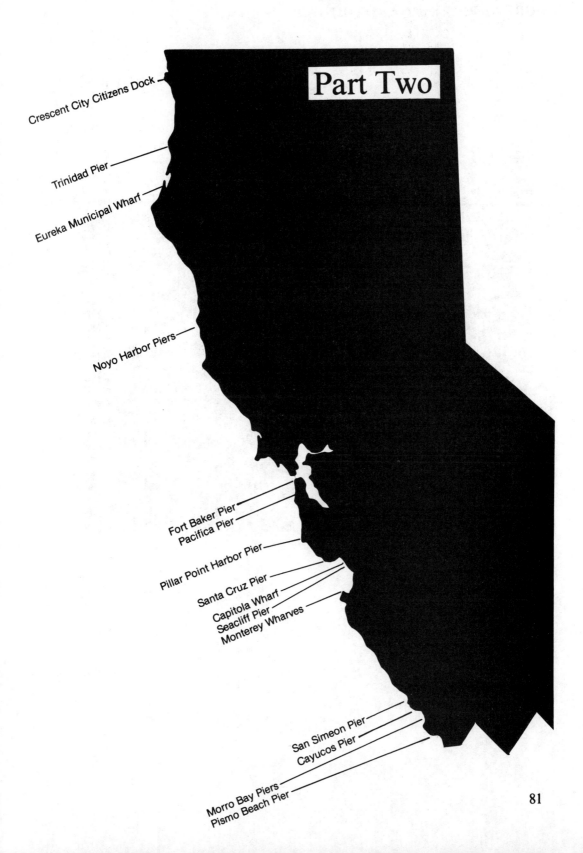

Crescent City Citizens Dock

Trinidad Pier

Eureka Municipal Wharf

Noyo Harbor Piers

Fort Baker Pier
Pacifica Pier

Pillar Point Harbor Pier

Santa Cruz Pier

Capitola Wharf
Seacliff Pier
Monterey Wharves

San Simeon Pier
Cayucos Pier

Morro Bay Piers
Pismo Beach Pier

Part Two

81

AVILA BEACH
and
PORT SAN LUIS PIERS

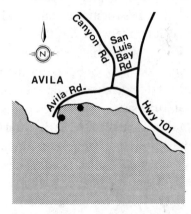

Funny how you can pass by a place a dozen times and never really see it. From the highway just south of San Luis Obispo, if you look out toward Point San Luis at the right moment, you'll see two piers. Avila (AH-vee-la) and San Luis piers live in the same cove: lying four or five miles from the main road, they're off the beaten track and used mostly by sportsfishermen and people who live nearby.

Port San Luis (originally Port Harford) is the deepsea fisherman's landfall, and Avila is Bikini City—or was, till winter storms ripped out the pier's center and left it closed off and dead, for the moment. But the two began as rivals, angling not for fishermen or suntanners but for a considerably bigger prize.

7:00 A.M. Avila, still, just waking up under gray, thick, low-hanging clouds; but along the horizon you can see a darker streak, that will be breaking up later. Against the pale calm water, Avila Pier is a dark skeleton, broken away in two places by winter storm waves. A pair of joggers on the beach, and two dogs running free, one galloping through the surf, drenching himself. PSL Pier lies across the water, just inside the point: the boats moored around it are beginning to gleam in the morning light.

Breakfast, Avila's Old Custom House: the flower-filled patio is still chilly, but the caged birds chitter and creek, going about their own business.

10:00 A.M. The sun is breaking through, there's color in the water, and PSL Pier is humming. The entrance to the pier is flanked by the Live Oak Boat Works, power saws whining, and an RV parking lot for sportsfishermen who can launch their trailered boats here. The electric hoist can handle up to 500 pounds, and the tackle shop near the base of the 1,370-foot pier also rents fishing equipment.

The pier lies snug in the lee of the point, and is further protected by a 2,160-foot breakwater. About 120 commercial and pleasure boats are moored here, going out for rockcod all year round, and salmon and albacore in season...most common sound hereabouts is the metallic gargling of a boat motor.

The end of the pier is crowned by a big peaked-roof shed, two stories, with a high square doorway like an old barn. Anything labeled Olde Port Inn has got to be a fake, right? Wrong. Once a railroad warehouse, the building remains from the days when narrow-gauge trains ran out here. A second-story restaurant has been built under the high roof along the west side, and a glassed-in deck with space heaters faces the point. You can drive out and park for the restaurant under the roof, if there's room. The outer end of the shed has no walls: swallows nest in the rafters, and the wind whistles down the open center.

Plenty of fishermen this morning, many using floats including kids' balloons, green, blue, pink bobbing on the water. Alongside the building a fishing boat unloads its catch, mountains of pale pink shrimp and several big rock cod, bright coral, their black round eyes popped out. Tails dragging, they're hauled straight into the wholesale fish market and flopped up on the sinks. The stacks of boxes outside proclaim *100% fresh—0% preservatives.* Today the retail fish market next door has, among other goodies, oysters, local prawns and whole albacore, and two kinds of smoked bonito, plain and sugar-smoked.

Eastward across the bay the view is rural California, tawny hills with a few live oaks widely spaced. That's where the first wharf was built here, east of Avila in 1855 at Cave Landing, beyond the little point. It stood in water so shallow that freight and passengers had to be brought ashore in lighters (surfboats), traveling on to San Luis Obispo by stagecoach.

In 1868 People's Wharf was built near the present-day Avila Pier, but it was vulnerable to heavy weather. The most protected location obviously was right here inside the point, so in 1873 John Harford built a 540-foot wharf on this spot, reached by narrow-gauge railway cars drawn by horses. When another shipping company built a rail line out to Avila, the battle was joined.

Rivalry of the Avila and Port Harford piers brought about a rate war, so that for a time passengers could travel first class from San Francisco to San Diego for five dollars, including meals. Building of the three-story Hotel Marre at the foot of Port Harford Wharf, by then lengthened to 1,500 feet, helped handle the growing traffic: by 1876 two trains ran daily each way from the bay to San Luis Obispo.

Hotel Marre, with its widow's walk overlooking the harbor, was a favorite honeymoon spot for years. It burned in 1936, in an electrical storm. Remains of the foundation can be seen behind the harbormaster's office at the foot of the pier.

The island incorporated in the breakwater is Whale Island, where a whaling station operated for a few seasons around 1874. Smith Island, inside the breakwater, was the home of Joe and Mattie Smith and their children in the 1880s. The breakwater itself, of rock blasted loose and barged down from Morro Rock, took about five years to build, from 1908 to 1913.

Among the new steamships ordered for the growing California shipping trade was the *Queen of the Pacific*, 2,727 tons, constructed in Philadelphia and then sailed around the Horn with a load of passengers. Arriving in Port Harford in August 1882, she was greeted by a special train of sightseers, who went aboard for a champagne buffet. A week later she went into service on the California Southern route, calling here at the wharf both ways.

At 2:00 A.M. on May 1, 1888, the *Queen* was fifteen miles north of Port Harford when she mysteriously began taking water in the engine room. While the crew manned the pumps, the captain steamed full speed for this port. The engines went dead 500 feet off the end of the wharf, and the ship sank in twenty-two feet of water, rolling over to a 60-degree list with one side exposed. (See graph.) All 125 passengers and the crew got to shore safely in lifeboats. Two days later divers found an open deadlight at the water line in the cargo hold: since competition between steamships and stagecoach lines for passengers was especially fierce just then, sabotage was strongly suggested.

The ship was pumped out and floated again, towed up to San Francisco, renovated and renamed simply *Queen*. She was not a lucky ship: in 1904 she burned at sea and was towed to San Francisco and rebuilt; burned at sea again in 1914 and was rebuilt once more in San Francisco, and was finally scrapped in Osaka, Japan, in 1935.

When the Southern Pacific Railway completed its coast line in 1901, that was the beginning of the end for Port Harford's passenger service—even though it continued till 1929, when the last passenger ship, the steamer *San Juan*, docked here. Oil had been found around Santa Maria, and the wharf was extended to accommodate oil tankers; but the rise of auto and passenger buses and the competition of standard gauge railways eventually ended the port's shipping career. In 1954 the Port San Luis Harbor District was formed, and in 1964 it bought and renovated the pier.

The little village of Avila has become a beach resort. After seventy years, the last train left Avila in 1941—a work train, taking up the tracks behind it. Six-block Front Street is lined with curio, saltwater taffy and fish-and-chips places, bars (Barbara's at the Beach has a nifty 1930s sign), and stands renting beach chairs and board.

This is certainly the place where SLO County kids go in the summer... brown bodies fragrant with suntan oil line the beach, and here and there a frisbee rises—

the beach is too sloped for volleyball. Beachgoers are self-segregated, teenagers left of the pier, young marrieds and little kids to the right; and around the point at old Cave Landing is the nude beach.

Plans are to rebuild Avila Pier "as soon as funds are available." The 1,570-foot wooden pier's working origins show in its broad outer end. And its pilings are obviously tree-trunks, their knots and twists giving the pier a hand-hewn look. "Yes, it's generally pretty quiet here," said the lady in the curio shop. "Like my brother says, it's the place for the newlywed and the nearly dead."

8:00 P.M. At the Olde Port Inn the dinner hour is in full swing. The water fades and vanishes, leaving the boats riding dim and ghostly at their moorings, and across the water the lights of Avila Beach come up, clusters of amber points. A pair of headlights, and another, along the shore road.

Earlier, around 5:00, you would've seen a solid line of cars inching along the two-lane road, going home from PG&E's Diablo Canyon plant—the entrance to the nuclear power plant lies just a few hundred yards from the foot of PSL Pier. And here and there on the beach and along the quiet shoreline, you'll see the tasteful brown-and-white signs telling you what radio frequency to dial if you should hear the three- to seven-minute warning siren. Diablo is a major local employer, stoutly defended by most local residents: thousands of others have come to protest its existence. One thing's for sure: they've put the place on the map.

PISMO BEACH PIER

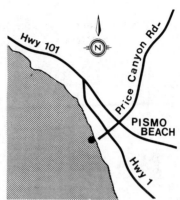

That beach. Pismo Beach Pier lies over the flattest sandy bottom on the coast, where the breakers roll on and on, six or seven lines of froth sliding in together. From here the beach and the dunes stretch southward for twenty-three miles; and you could drive five miles without a break, rolling easily along the broad band of wet, hard-packed sand, and stop to dig some fat white Pismo clams, heavy in the hand.

We knew that the Pismo Pier had fairly well survived the winter of '83, but we didn't know that El Niño had scoured away most of that wonderful beach. Approaching the foot of the pier on a July afternoon, you could see nothing but two huge heaps of sand, with a footpath angling between. When the sea had eaten all the beach, it attacked the concrete seawall at the foot of the pier, partly undermining it and breaking away a chunk at one end. The Army Corps of Engineers had nearly finished building a massive new seawall of heavy ribbed metal.

The pier beyond is its old rough and ready self, almost unchanged...deeply weathered, and mottled gray-white by the droppings of uncounted seabirds, the heavy wooden planks thump underfoot, many of them loose and shifting. This pier is high above the water, surprisingly long-legged for such a shallow surf. The outer third is gone, and with it the furthermost tackle and bait building. The remaining tackle stand also sells snacks and beer and a few curios, shell necklaces and the like.

Out on the end an aging young buck lounges on a pile of new planks drinking a beer and joking with fishermen leaning along the rail, fairly well covering the sign: *No fishing on this side dawn to dusk.* The shrieks of excited kids drift up from that lazy swath of surf, where they can still wade out for yards and yards and jump and thrash in the endless green scallops rolling in for about a mile. Plenty of kids fishing too, and strollers and tourists—Pismo has been a central California resort, the lungs and maybe the safety valve for inlanders for nearly a hundred years.

In 1881 the Meherin brothers of nearby Arroyo Grande built Pismo Wharf to ship out their produce. They made their wharf 1,600 feet long and twenty-seven feet above low water, with a hand-car track to take goods out to the end. In 1882, thirty-seven vessels called at the wharf. The beach was rapidly becoming popular

In horse and buggy days, Pismo Pier was already the central coast's place to go for entertainment.

for "bathing and pleasure," as they said then, and early vacationers drove buggies along its hard sands.

In those days clams were so plentiful that farmers sometimes plowed them up to use as fertilizer. The Chumash Indians before them also dug the clams, and gathered the globs of tar which sometimes floated up on the beach, using it to waterproof their baskets. *Pismo* is a Chumash word for tar.

The builder of the Hotel El Pizmo spelled it that way because he liked it better: you may still find this spelling for the town's name on early maps.

A dance pavilion was built at the foot of the pier, and a tent city for summer campers flourished around it from 1895 into the 1920s. This was evidently a good-time town from the beginning. "Saloons and the things that go with them tend to draw a certain element, and the place suffers in consequence," a 1917 writer dryly declared. Motorcycle riding on the beach became popular, and visitors could also take a plane ride with ex-World War I pilots who landed their light planes on the beach.

Pismo clams were harvested commercially from 1916 to 1947, an estimated 100,000 pounds a year. Amateur clammers took more: they've taken as many as two million clams (4,000,000 pounds) from a four-mile stretch in two and a half months, leaving (alas) an equal number exposed to die. Currently the limit is ten clams apiece: they must be at least five inches across, and any not taken should be covered with sand again so they'll survive.

Downtown Pismo still has a temporary, throwaway feeling, surprising considering the town's age—businesses that come and go, boarded-up storefronts and weedy lots in among the cafes and curio shops, the rollerskating rink and the country western bar advertising live music all day Sunday. Kids in cars and trucks with booming speakers cruise up and down pumping out waves of sound, celebrating youth and endless summer.

A parking lot faces the pier, and at its south corner, the foot of Hinds Street is a ramp onto the beach. Although riding on the beach is a longstanding attraction for tourists (and revenue), residents have been divided over whether to let it continue. Some object to "one-hand drinking and one-hand driving" and "performers who execute 'doughnuts,' and 'wheelies' and the game of 'chicken' with people and other vehicles," and have periodically succeeded in banning vehicles from Pismo's section of the sand. But right now it's not much of a problem; not till El Niño and the mighty tides and currents of the sea bring back the beach.

MORRO BAY PIERS

The Rock. On a foggy morning you can't see all of Morro Rock...opposite the waterfront its great bulk rises, but only the base is visible, seamed and particolored granite with tufts of clinging vegetation: the rest is hidden. The maze of masts and rigging sharpens, the sportboats and purse seiners moored along the docks as the light blooms on paint and metal. Colors revive in the pale sun and the shape advances, bigger even than you remembered; huge.

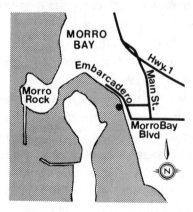

Morro Bay's three public piers all lie toward the north end of the harbor, opposite the Rock, with the mouth of the channel curving between it and them. The mighty rock helped form the harbor, and shapes it still.

The upcoast pier, backed by the steady rumbling of the PG&E plant, is short and broad, with a 190-foot stem and a wide end, 395 feet across; only a few feet above the water, and more like a dock than most piers.

On this morning its outer edge was lined solid with fishing boats, their long nets of blue, black, green wound into high piles on their sterns. On several of the boats, crewmen were mending the nets. Here a man worked rhythmically, measuring the distance between knots with a long stick polished to a gloss by much handling. The cork and blown-glass floats that once buoyed the nets are long gone, replaced by a string of hot-pink plastic floats like children's beach balls.

The north end of the pier is reserved for the Coast Guard: a cutter moored there is opened regularly to visitors. The rest of the pier was edged by fishermen, and a few people crabbing. . . the passage of many feet has worn down the dock, so that the harder knots stick up like map contours.

The next pier, a little way south and of the same proportions, a broad, shallow T, was deserted except for pigeons.

The waterfront stretches along the foot of a bluff southward for a mile or so, lined with restaurants and shops and sportfishing landings. Party boats go out mostly for bottom fish, and sometimes barracuda, white sea bass, salmon or albacore. There are slips and moorings for more than 220 commercial and 184 pleasure boats, and in winter the harbor shelters many of those tied up at Port San Luis during the summer.

Clam taxis are available at Morro Bay Marina, to take you sightseeing in the harbor or across the channel to dig clams along the sand spit. The immense sand spit which forms the outer wall of the harbor stretches up five miles from the south, with fifty-foot-high dunes in some spots. It's now part of Montaña de Oro State Park, whose entrance is on the coast south of Morro Bay Lagoon. Onshore winds carrying sand from the spit have in fact partially filled in the big lagoon.

About midway along the waterfront, at the point where the Embarcadero jogs, lies Morro Bay's third pier, certainly the smallest on the California coast. Its stem is 4' x 78', ending in a 12' x 16' platform with a lamp at each corner. The city built it and the floating docks on each side to provide more fiishing space and a public window on the bay, and has recently added a pocket park at the foot of the pier.

Five benches, two picnic tables and a wedge of lawn where you can lie and contemplate the rock; all bordered by a swag of chain, with pairs of monster foot-high links as uprights. In the center of the little park a block of granite supporting a 7,000-pound anchor bears a plaque with the names of twenty-eight Morro fishermen lost at sea—among them two Santoses, two Pierces, two Cefalus and four Fannings.

Morro Rock, chief creator of sand spit and harbor, has at the same time made navigation here difficult. Until recent years, Morro Rock was an island. Named Moro (later Morro) by the Spaniards because it reminded them of the head of a turbaned Moor, the landmark did not become the site of a settlement until 1870, when Franklin Riley settled here and established the embarcadero, building a wharf to ship out local produce. Many of the eucalyptus in town date from that time, when thousands of blue gum seedlings and seeds from Tasmania were planted as windbreaks and to hold the blowing sand.

In 1873 Riley built a second wharf out into fourteen-foot water, and a warehouse on the bluff where the Log Cabin Motel is now. To move goods easily, an inclined chute was extended from the warehouse over the road on a trestle and across the wharf. The lip of the chute went into the ship's hold, and was hinged to accommodate itself to the rise and fall of the tides; and a bit of kerosene on each sack of barley made it slide better. A railroad pier was also built, and shipments of redwood and pine brought in from Santa Cruz.

In 1874 the town's first harbor troubles developed. Steamship lines refused to dock here regularly because of a general belief that the harbor was unsafe, and farmers with perishables began to ship from Cayucos instead, though some independent ships did make the stop.

The problem was that Morro Bay's two entrances could only be taken with the right combination of winds and tides; and both channels were feared by schooner captains. With a northwest wind, they waited to come in on a full tide through the north channel—which was deep enough, but close to the Rock. In the south channel, such a wind would be blocked by the Rock. To go out by the north channel, they wanted a north wind and an out-going tide.

The south channel was entered on an incoming tide with a south wind. They could leave the bay by the south channel on a north wind only if the tide was ebbing, because the tide by itself would be strong enough to carry them even though the wind was blocked.

And the harbor's reputation wasn't improved by what happened one day in February 1877. The schooner *Mary Taylor* was hove to north of the Rock with a load of lumber, waiting to come in: the seas were rough, with tremendous swells.

The local harbor pilot, the Reverend. Alden Bradford Spooner, was a minister who also farmed. Born in Maine, by the time he was eighteen Spooner had already sailed on the frigate *Constitution*, also known as *Old Ironsides*, or so the story goes. Spooner put out from the embarcadero in his small boat to pilot the *Mary Taylor* in. He got through the north channel safely, but as he neared Pilot Rock his boat capsized. Spooner's body was never recovered.

Extensive quarrying of the 576-foot rock, which covers forty acres, began in the 1890s. Tons of rock were blasted loose and loaded onto barges from a pier built out on its south side, before the townfolk realized that the Rock could eventually be destroyed. Much of it was towed downcoast to form the Port San Luis breakwater, and it's also part of several local buildings, among them Dutch's Criddle House.

By 1912 the shallow harbor channel had filled considerably, further hampering shipping. But the town was becoming popular with summer visitors escaping the San Joaquin Valley heat, and hundreds camped on the beach north of town. "Morro is now quite a lively little town," a visitor wrote in 1917. "No saloons are allowed, and naturally only a good class of people come to Morro."

In 1930 a jetty was built between the rock and the mainland, in hopes that tidal currents would be strengthened enough to scour the entrance channel and keep it open. But sand rapidly built out along the north side of the jetty, filling in the angle between mainland and rock, and the wind began to blow this sand over the jetty, forming shoals in the harbor. At the same time, the altered current began to move the north end of the giant sand spit landward.

To prevent further damage, two breakwaters were then built; one extending south from the rock, and the other west from near the end of the sand spit. These keep the harbor open: but during heavy seas the waves sometimes break across the entrance. A 1958 newspaper photo shows mammoth waves crashing over the spit and filling the bay. From the piers you can see the red markers outlining the channel, which must be regularly dredged by the Army Corps of Engineers to be maintained.

The stretch of Highway 1 from San Simeon to Carmel opened in 1937, after eighteen years' labor and a cost of $10 million and some lives: its popularity has brought more tourists to Morro Bay, to fish and camp and explore the dunes and the harbor. At sunset the restaurants along the water are full...the sun is engulfed by a fog bank out beyond Morro Rock, leaving streaks of gold and a sky of subdued live-shrimp pink above the sand spit.

Over the ocean a flight of birds is heading somewhere for the night—Morro is a bird sanctuary, there are all kinds here. A flock of gulls wheels above the masts and then settles rocking on the gray water beside the spit, and lights begin to come on, a line of them marking the road out to the rock, and the greenish lights on the little pier. A strange thing: above the crown of the Rock in the clear evening a wispy cloud forms, created by some updraft...steadily blowing inland but at the same time persisting, maintaining its position—just hanging there.

Cayucos Pier has a distinct rise halfway out. The rounded, nearly treeless hills are characteristic of this section of the coast.

Sunday sail, never fail,
Friday sail, ill luck and gale.
                    —Old Mother Goose

CAYUCOS PIER

Neat, quiet Cayucos (Ki-YOO-cos) Pier centers Estero Bay, upcoast from Morro about four miles and a whole world away. It's a plain wooden pier, cross-planked and well-maintained, its outer end rising and widening rather like the back of a spoon. No structures, tackle stand or curios, no tourists; just a few fishermen and a couple of local strollers up from the bathing beach alongside the pier.

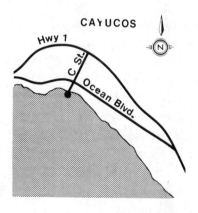

You can rent skiffs nearby and go out for bottom fish, and troll for salmon when they come in close enough: there's a boat launching ramp a quarter mile north of here. Beyond the beach in both directions, the shore becomes rocky. The central coast is popular with skindivers, for spearfishing and taking abalone—even red abalone can still be found sometimes. Al's Sporting Goods on the corner of Ocean Boulevard, the town's main street just back of the pier, has diving gear for rent.

Cayucos (pop. 2,104) is overshadowed now by Morro Bay: but it wasn't always so. The town was founded by Captain James Cass, who built a deep-water wharf here in 1875 to ship out dairy products, hides and beef. His pier was 940 feet, with a 40′ x 60′ outer end, and piles of Cambria pine. Trade grew, till at one time there was a 700-foot hitching rail outside the warehouse beside the wharf, with as many as 125 teams hitched up on "butter days" when farmers brought in their produce.

When early skippers decided that Morro's harbor was too dangerous, Cayucos became a regular stop of the Pacific Steamship Company's southern coast route, which stopped at San Simeon, Cayucos and Port Harford every four days. Usually, that is...sometimes the steamers bypassed Cayucos, leaving butter, eggs and other perishables standing on the wharf. Cayucans protested mightily, with little effect.

The abalone, so abundant then along the coast, were gathered here by Japanese and canned for several seasons, the cannery operating between May and September. In 1917, for example, the cannery shipped 6,000 cases of abalone, mostly for export.

The big peaked-roof building at the foot of the pier is the Veterans Memorial Building, with the town library occupying a back corner, and a patio around on the north side with two big public barbeques, metal grills suspended over the fire pits, raised and lowered by wheels and chains. On Fourth of July Cayucos usually holds a big celebration complete with parade and barbeque.

A block back of the pier you'll see an unpainted Victorian house weathered to a warm brown. This was Captain Cass's home, built of lumber shipped from San Francisco and constructed when he built his wharf more than a hundred years ago. It was originally light buff with brown trim, and had a front porch, ornate Victorian woodwork, gardens and a clipped cypress hedge, the whole enclosed by a picket fence.

The balance of Ocean Boulevard is a mixture of old false fronts, utilitarian stucco buildings from the recent past, and a few buildings which have been restored and made into antique shops and restaurants, like the Way Station. The rest of the town slopes uphill four or five blocks to the highway, with treeless sunburnt hills beyond.

Cayucos was named by the Spaniards, who saw Indians out in the bay straddling boats of reeds or tules, paddling with their feet; and were reminded of the *cayucos* used by Venezuelan Indians. On this bright afternoon the wind is up, cutting across from the point, and two windsurfers wrestle with their sails out where the Indians and the schooners once went about their business.

Two painters are working their way down each side of the pier laying a coat of fresh white paint on the railings. South of the pier a hundred yards or so, a strange sight—a long streak of birds, a dark rough patch of them as long as the pier and parallel with it; hundreds riding the water, more rising, coming and settling—they must be feeding. Does it happen often?

"Yes, pretty often," one of the painters says. "Seem to be more birds than usual today. Closer in, too." Beyond the birds, across the deep blue water, stand those two landmarks; the smokestacks of the PG&E plant, and the rocky dome of El Morro.

SAN SIMEON PIER

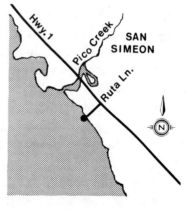

San Simeon is a tall, narrow, white-railinged pier in a peaceful country cove sheltered by the wooded point to the north. Piers in Central and Northern California were often so situated, in the lee of an upcoast point which offered some protection from the prevailing winds and waves.

At the head of the pier, a grove of eucalyptus provides rustling shade for the lawn alongside with picnic tables and barbeques—this is a state park, with a charge for day use. From here you can see the parking lot above the highway, used by visitors touring Hearst Castle, and in the distance La Cuesta Encantada itself, solitary among the golden hills.

The pier, level with the top of the low bluff, goes straight out for about thirty feet and then angles left. Dozens of swallows nest under the pier, darting out in pursuit of insects. Children fishing here were catching small red snappers, and periodically getting their hooks caught in the kelp which drifted in patches south of the pier. There's a launch for trailered boats on the pier, and four or five boats were moored in the cove.

97

On the outer end of the pier stairs lead down to the floating dock where passengers board the all-day boat operating during the summer. Virg's Fish'n at the foot of the pier sells tackle, and Irene Meyer, who lives in Fresno during the winter, comes over to help run the office in the summer.

Downcoast the beach gives way to rocky shoreline. All the property in this area except for Sebastian's Store and the government lighthouse at Piedras Blancas belonged to William Randolph Hearst, which is why it has remained undeveloped. The sandy beach at the foot of the pier curves around toward the point, past San Simeon's few buildings. On the ocean front are two windowless storage buildings and a square Spanish-style structure, white with arches and a red tile roof, slightly lopsided. A stream enters the ocean at the end of the beach nearest the point, creating a secluded cove sometimes used for nude bathing.

The present pier, built in 1957 by San Luis Obispo County, became part of the state's Hearst Memorial Park in 1971. The original wharf served a shore-whaling station set up in 1852 by whale-watchers who observed the migration of the gray whales from the headlands; when they spotted one blowing, they put out in small boats. The village on San Simeon Point grew to include a general store, a blacksmith shop, barber shop and saloon, and another wharf built alongside the point to serve sailing ships carrying travelers and goods.

Senator George Hearst bought San Simeon Rancho in 1865 and built a new thousand-foot railroad wharf in 1878. During the wharf's first year it shipped out butter, tallow, beef hides, grain, seaweed, abalone and 169 flasks of quicksilver from the mercury mines in the area. At extreme low tide you can still see the remains of Hearst's pier. But the whaling industry declined and so did the village, and the general store which is now Sebastian's was put on skids and hauled by horses to its present location.

William Randolph Hearst became sole owner of San Simeon Ranch in 1919, and began the lifelong construction of his castle. All the building materials and many of the furnishings were landed here: a nonstop collector of art, Hearst bought about a million dollars worth a year for several years, packing his warehouses with paintings, statuary, doorways, mantels, china, silver. A resident said that the warehouses along the shore are still full of antiques and art treasures Hearst bought, and they're opened up periodically, to "stock up at the castle."

If you follow the road past the pier to the village, you'll see several Spanish-style houses with red tile roofs, originally built for Hearst employees. Sebastian's is still doing business as a general store, with fresh meat and staples, postcards and picnic supplies. It's also the local post office: the mailboxes are in back. High up on the side wall are implements from the whaling station—harpoons, a big pierced spoon used for skimming during the rendering of the whale oil.

MONTEREY WHARVES

When you get to Monterey, remember that there are two piers here. Fisherman's Wharf lives by the streaming multitudes of tourists who come looking for traces of its colorful past; but today the big gray pier across the harbor, Municipal Wharf, is where the fishing business really goes on.

The first pier was built when Monterey was still the capital of Alta California and a part of Mexico. This spot has seen whalers, lateen-sailed salmon boats, Teddy Roosevelt's Great White Fleet and the big purse seiners of the sardine fleet from the glory years immortalized by John Steinbeck.

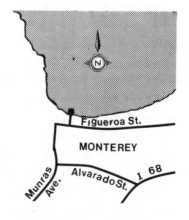

The main stem of Fisherman's Wharf is walled in with souvenir shops, restaurants and fish markets: diners have good views, but only toward the outer end does the pedestrian actually see the harbor. Best time of day here for me is morning, when the fish sellers are arranging their glistening goods and the big wooden boxes of crushed ice rumble over the bumpy asphalt. Beside the seafood restaurant out on the end a staircase leads up to an observation deck, with telescopes, which gives you a good view of the harbor. From the point on your left the Coast Guard jetty, built in 1934 and recently lengthened, extends its arm to protect the boats moored inside. It hasn't always succeeded: big storms in 1943 and again in '53 drove dozens of boats onshore and demolished them.

Today there's a marina between the two piers, with launching ramps and berths for 367 boats behind a concrete sea wall parallel to the beach. The bigger commercial boats are moored around the end of Fisherman's.

Westward beyond the breakwater lies Cannery Row, once alive with the stink, smoke and clatter of the canneries and their docks. Now the remodeled Row caters to tourists, with restaurants and shops selling crafts and carvings, seascapes and metal sculptures of old fishing piers.

Fisherman's has sprouted a second tip, edged with boxes of red geraniums, where diners can take the air and enjoy the view in three directions. The adjoining finger wharf extending east has itself two T extensions parallel with the main pier. On one of them the big observation diving bell that used to plunge down thirty feet with a great splash seems to be fatally immobilized: its paint is blistered and rusting and the platform supporting it charred from a fire.

And the sea lions are out early, too; one of them circles between the piers barking non-stop like the neighbor's crazy dog down the street, while two others hang around waiting to see what his begging will bring them.

Alongside Sammy's Sportfishing the partyboats are tied up, and around back the lines are loaded with gunnysacks, hung out to dry against the deep red wall. From here the pier's haphazard charms are more evident; diners double-deck moving ghostly behind the big reflecting windows, the weathered buildings zigzag on their pilings, seabirds, a scruffy boat alongside with its decks all white, crusted with fish-scales.

One of the T's has stairways down to a lower level where kids go to fish, and you can see dinghies pulled up and hanging in the maze of pilings. Straight out, somewhere near the end of the breakwater, another sea lion has begun to bark.

Monterey, sheltered by the northward curve of Point Pinos, was made capital of Alta California by the Spaniards in 1775. Describing the port in *Two Years Before the Mast*, in 1835 Richard Henry Dana noted that

"The harbour, too, is a good one, being subject to only one bad wind from the north: and though the holding-ground is not the best, yet I heard of but one vessel being driven ashore here. That was a Mexican brig, which went ashore a few months before our arrival, and was a wreck, all the crew but one being drowned."

Ten years later the first wharf in California was built at this spot by Thomas Larkin, a merchant who was also the first and only U.S. consul to California. Larkin's wharf was built of stone quarried by military deserters, Indians and civil prisoners—1,500 cartloads of it, at $1 a load. The pilings cost him $4 apiece, his total expense being $8,000.

Portuguese whalers set up a whaling station at Monterey in 1854, towing in their catch and rendering the whales on the beach: by 1857 there were three whaling companies here. A visitor in 1861 found the beach white with whalebones, with clouds of vultures fattening on the decayed carcasses. Chinese fishermen discovered salmon to be had in the bay, and in 1853 established a fishing colony which grew to around 300. The salmon were salted and shipped out in wooden tubs: in 1907 in the month of June alone they packed 210,000 pounds of salmon.

In these early years the fish were so plentiful that they were sometimes netted from the beach alongside the wharf. Around 1895 one P.E. Booth came to town, and began experimenting with new canning methods. He dried sardines in the sun, hand-flaked them and packed them in hand-soldered cans. In 1902 he built

Wharf No. 2, Monterey's Municipal Pier, under construction in 1926.

Monterey's first cannery, just west of the present Fishermen's Wharf. That first season he packed 300 cans of sardines: the second, 3,000.

An Italian fisherman, Pietro Ferrante, in 1905 introduced Mediterranean *lampara* nets, designed to encircle a whole school of fish. (The name, from the Italian *lampo*—lightning—described the netting and hauling done in one swoop.) More canneries went up, and nets and boats grew larger, till a crew of six was bringing in as much as twenty-five tons of sardines in a night.

Best fishing was on dark, moonless nights, when fishermen could spot the phosphorescent schools of fish. In the early days they soaked the big cotton nets in a tanning solution to strengthen them: later, they switched to tarring the nets.

World War I gave local fishing a big boost, as the government began buying canned sardines to ship around the world. Canneries operated around the clock, with workers living nearby in shacks and tents: by 1918 there were nine canneries working. Each had its own distinctive whistle and, day or night, when the boats came in the cannery workers listened for the whistle from their own plant summoning them. By this time they were cooking the fish in the can, packed with chili-pepper for seasoning.

On a stormy morning in March 1923, the largest load of sardines yet—20,000 cases—was standing on the end of the pier waiting to be loaded onto the *S.S. Antonio* standing alongside, when heavy groundswells shoved the ship into the pier. A 132-foot section collapsed, dumping 10,000 cases into the bay. Most of them were recovered, to a chorus of "twice-caught sardines" jokes by the locals, and the pier rebuilt, extended, and the present side pier added.

In 1929 four million cases of fish were canned; and that year the fishing industry saw what was called a revolutionary improvement—the purse seiner. Big diesel-powered boats mechanically set huge nets 200-220 fathoms long, encircled a school and then drew together the bottom of the net like a purse, so that no fish could escape. These boats could travel hundreds of miles and bring back 140-150 tons of fish.

Through the '30s and the early '40s the sardine catch grew, and townfolk called the throat-clutching stink of rotting fish "the smell of prosperity." By 1945 the 100-plus fishing fleet, 84 of them purse seiners, kept Monterey's nineteen canneries and twenty reduction plants working to capacity, canning 234,613 tons of sardines that year, in total tonnage ranking below only Stavanger, Norway, and Hull, England. This was the sardine capital of the world.

And then—something happened. The next year the catch was only 143,282 tons: the year after, it dropped to 26,618 tons. Where did the sardines go?

Over-fishing, some said; pollution, changes in current, temperature, said others. Fishermen had one more good year, 1950, with a catch of 130,000 tons. By 1952 the canneries were closing, selling their equipment to companies in Venezuela and South Africa. The only cannery operating today is packing squid.

Ironically, 1945 was also the year Steinbeck's *Cannery Row* was published, celebrating "the poem and the stink and the grating noise...the dream" of life along the Row. It drew the tourists to Monterey, to see for themselves; and the townspeople followed after, naturally enough, seeking the silver in this throng to replace their swimming silver, now departed.

Fisherman's Wharf, known locally as Wharf No. 1, was so busy by the 1920s that the 1,750-foot Wharf No. 2 was built in 1926 as a cargo pier. The warehouse out on the end now houses several fish buyers and a processing plant. Most dependable catch in Monterey today is squid, or *calamari*, netted by the ton in huge writhing balls, brought in and scooped into the hopper with the big round brail nets you'll see hanging along the wall.

Largest part of the catch is canned and sent overseas, but the domestic market is growing. The abalone steak was first popularized in Monterey; but with the price of abalone $18 a pound and rising, local restaurants have made squid a specialty; in Italian dishes, calamari and eggplant—and you can get squid and eggs for breakfast at Grandma's kitchen on Fremont.

Parking meters march up the starboard rail of Wharf No. 2, with fishermen between pulled up close, folding chairs and tackle boxes marking out their Sunday territories. You know where you are: there's water all around, and a great view of the old wharf opposite, a maze of weathered pilings and cockeyed roofs. The morning fog blurring the ridges of the low dark-firred hills is melting away and the colors grow, easy as sunrise, blue water and the boats swaying, and that cool brilliant air fills the eyes and lungs and spirit.

A clump of brown kelp rocks gently...and suddenly we make out the sleek head, eyes closed, and the paws; a sea otter clasping a branch to his chest, snoozing in the pale gold of morning.

On the port rail a backed-up pickup truck spills a new black fishing net onto the deck of a fishing boat riding below with its motor running—two men standing on the boat, swaying as it rolls, carry on a laughing conversation in some Slavic language with the man on the dock, while the three Viet deckhands catch the streaming folds and coil them into a rising mound on the stern. Done; the cover thrown over, wrestled into place and lashed down. Up on the pier a fat roll of hundred-dollar bills appears, they're counted off and change hands.

On the boat the man at the wheel pulls away from the wharf; the deckhands in their separate spots lean back expressionless, and one lights a cigarette. Twenty years from now maybe some Viet novelist will tell us what it was like, working on a fishing boat out of Monterey back in the '80s....

SEACLIFF PIER

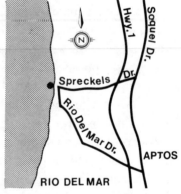

The first time you see that improbable hulk, you blink and look again...a long, low, gray ship, half-submerged, lying perpendicular to the beach and pointing out to sea, its bow cracked away and tilted up. The good cement ship *Palo Alto* rests on the ocean bottom about 400 feet off Seacliff Beach and connected to it by a wooden pier. Hard to imagine it ever afloat.

From the bluff above, the pier is a hybrid; wide, busy wooden floor becoming curving boat deck and then rubble, and that curving prow inhabited only by birds. Walking along the pier, you come to a wall of fencing and a doorway and go down several shallow steps onto the ship itself.

Part of the ship's thick, curving chest-high railing of pink cement remains, but farther out the railing has been replaced by sections of chain-link fencing, so the smaller kids can see, too—there are lots of children fishing; it's definitely a family pier.

A tall fence separates the pier from the shattered forward deck just where its wheelhouse began: only part of the roof is left. Fallen-away chunks of concrete expose thick iron rods and bundles of cable, broken and twisted like giant rusty spaghetti. The bow, a whitening island now, belongs to the gulls and pelicans and the black snake-necked cormorants. The sea surges between...in the green shadows just below us, the moving water sucks and slops through half-submerged doorways.

A concrete ship just seems—unlikely. They had been designed by 1910, but World War I and the wartime shortage of steel provided a good reason to actually build such a ship. The *Palo Alto* was one of three built by the U.S. Navy in Oakland. Intended to be an oil tanker, she wasn't quite finished when the war ended. And then she remained docked at Oakland until 1929, when the Cal-Nevada Company bought her. Her only ocean voyage was the fifteen-hour trip to this spot, towed by the Red Stack tugboat *Sea Scout*.

A decisive mooring: her seacocks were opened, and the 435-foot ship filled and settled to the bottom. The pier was built then, and a cafe in the ship's superstructure, a dance floor on the main deck, a fifty-four foot heated swimming pool amidships, and carnival booths on the afterdeck. She was finally launched on her new career in the summer of 1930—not the best of years for a maiden enterprise. After two seasons the company went broke; and in the winter of 1931-32, a severe storm cracked the ship and began the damage which continues with every storm.

Shortly thereafter, Seacliff Beach became part of the California park system. The ship sits alongside two miles of straight sand beaches, a popular camping area. However, signs on the bluff warn *Danger—Rip currents, Deep holes, No lifeguard*. Even on busy summer days the beach doesn't seem overcrowded, because it's long and narrow.

A covered area at the foot of the pier has several picnic tables, and other tables and barbeques nearby are shaded by the big pine and eucalyptus trees growing along the base of the cliff. The bait-tackle-snack shop on the wooden pier is open on weekends all year round, every day in summer.

Out on the ship, some excitement: along the right-hand side of the hull, a pink skiff pulls up with a six-foot blue shark sticking out of it, and a crowd collects, watching as the shark is hoisted over the railing and dumped on the deck. Now and again it thrashes, clearing a space with the arc of its tail. The kids are especially interested in its teeth.

A little later we saw the big blue brought down to the foot of the pier stuffed in a market cart, its eyes and stomach popped out, and watched it being loaded in the back of a little truck and hauled away to a local fish market. And back up the zig zag flight of 150 wooden steps to the overflow parking lot on top of the bluff. Through the trees you get a bird's eye view of the pier and the good ship *Palo Alto*—fifteen hours at sea, and fifty years aground with a deckload of landlubbers.

CAPITOLA WHARF

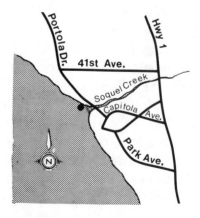

Capitola—absurd name for this charming little spot, with a pier perfectly situated to enjoy its human dimensions. But more than the scale; a lucky combination of elements. Your normal gray morning...the cheerful restaurant out on the end of the pier, swaying regularly, has granola with bananas on the menu; imagine.

A rowing shell moves across from the point, its oarsmen taking advantage of the morning calm to get in some practice. And on the beach hundreds of people in bright colors appear, with more coming every minute. A stream of runners pouring over the gray bridge and into the little downtown—it's the Wharf-to-Wharf Run from Santa Cruz, and everybody in the county must be in it, graybeards to eight-year-olds.

From out here, old Capitola is a juicy eye-filling wedge, with the beach the rim of it, curving around a lagoon perfect for swimming or floating on an air mattress—in the rainy season the river cuts through, but in summertime the sand fills across again. The opposite bank is lined with one-story buildings, restaurants with big outdoor decks that look across the little lagoon and beach to the pier.

Tip of the wedge is somewhere up-river, lost in the thick shadowy green, and then your eye goes up to the high railway trestle spanning the river, and across to the right where peak-roofed wooden houses climb the grassy bluff above the point, a few rocks and a bit of brilliant green moss exposed at low tide.

The wharf itself, damaged by storms in '78 and opened recently, is cross-planked and beginning to weather, with a bicycle rack, and comfortable benches at intervals, some set in small bays. You can rent one of the bright orange boats and motor—there's a hoist—or a wind-surfer, or go out on the half-day boat. There's a free tram running from the parking lots on top of the bluff down to the end of the pier, very useful: on weekends especially the town is jammed, and parking impossible.

The restaurant on the end has a staircase to the roof, and from up here you can see the ragged planking where the latest winter storms ripped away several feet of the deck.

That colorful pile at the foot of the pier is the Capitola Venetian, a mixture of apartments and motel; three single-story tiers of stucco painted salmon, ochre, green and buff, roofed in red tile. The stucco was troweled on in semi-circle scallops, and cast plaster dolphins and amphorae and Medusa's heads are painted contrasting colors.

Built during the 1920s, the Venetian has nine doorways carved in Venetian and Capitolan themes. . . a scene from Othello and two from Byron's poems, the Lion of St. Mark, the bridge over Soquel Creek, gondolas moored at Capitola Wharf. The manager told us about the particular wave that wrecked the corner apartment in '83.

The Capitola Wharf has stood here at the foot of Wharf Road since 1857, when it was known as Soquel Landing. Porter's Tannery in Soquel, just inland, by 1865 was producing enough leather every month to make 3,000 pairs of boots, and shipped the leather out to San Quentin, where it was worked into boots by the prisoners.

By the 1860s this spot was already attracting visitors escaping the heat of inland valleys, and in 1869 Camp Capitola was established on the east side of the creek. The name—ah, yes. The year before, the residents of Soquel had been seized by the desire to have their town named the state capitol: this is the only result.

Campers used the grounds free, only buying their provisions from the manager. They bathed in the sea in groups which gathered at 11:00 and at 3:00, summoned by the ringing of a bell, and waded into the surf in a great chain, hanging onto a rope attached to a float. And they fished: by the 1890s, as many as fifty boats moored around the wharf to take fishermen out after salmon.

In 1884 came the skating rink; by 1895 the three-story Capitola Hotel. That same year the Garlach Wave Motor Company built a wave-powered electric generator on the end of the wharf, intended to convert the force of the changing tides to motive power for an electric monorail connecting Capitola with Santa Cruz. The wave motor was a failure, but Capitola did get its electric railway to Santa Cruz in 1904.

By the '20s the town had become Capitola-by-the-Sea, a year-round resort for the family trade, with dancing at the Hawaiian Gardens and outdoor fun at The Chutes, a slide into the lagoon. In 1923 Highway 17 connected the coast with valley areas, and began the era of weekend traffic jams over the summit.

Through the '50s Capitola was a typical beach resort, with a merry-go-round, pinball machines and a bowling alley. But it nearly lost its beach when the Santa Cruz Yacht Harbor was built and stopped the southward movement of sand, depositing it beside the jetty instead. To repair the damage, Capitola built the 250-foot rock groin you see, hauling in 5,500 tons of rock and 2,000 truckloads of sand to restore its beach.

The amusements are gone now, replaced by shops and restaurants along the Esplanade with passageways to the beach between them, a protected observation area at the ocean end, and plenty of elegant handicrafts and clothing for sale. Sailboats come around the point from Santa Cruz, and downcoast you can just make out the sunken ship, blending into the shoreline.

Nightfall; a family with a portable barbeque is cooking their dinner on the sand, blankets marking off their living space. From the bluff above, the little lights come up along the coast and all the way around to a cluster that must be Monterey... Capitola itself is a dark rim enclosing those lights so nicely spaced they must be streetlights.

SANTA CRUZ PIER

Dedication of the present Santa Cruz Pier, on Dec. 5, 1914. Casino-amusement zone on the beach has its own "pleasure pier"; remains of the earlier Railroad Pier are just visible at left.

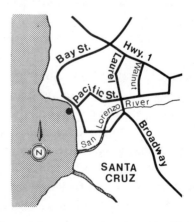

Santa Cruz Pier lies inside the upper end of Monterey Bay, that curve of coast so open that the Spaniards who came after its discoverer, Viscaino, didn't recognize it. The 2,745-foot pier faces south, and looks across an expanse of water to a swath of beach and the only surviving amusement park on the California coast, anchored at this end by the massive domed Casino, at the other by that fanciful construction all angles and curves folding back on itself, white girders and red track—the Giant Dipper, one of the last wooden roller coasters.

In contrast to the nostalgic pleasures opposite, the pier is strictly contemporary, on its outer half carrying a string of curio and tackle shops, fish markets and seafood restaurants all housed in simple block buildings painted in neutral colors, with few signs and no indication of the pier's long and lively past. Shops are grouped along the upcoast edge of the pier: when it was rebuilt in 1977, they were restricted to one story with a minimum of six feet between buildings, to keep the ocean visible. But out toward the end the skyline is broken now by a livelier pair of new buildings in warm varnished woods, almost finished; two stories, peaked and angled, with an elevated deck and walkway, and big windows that let strollers look through it to the shoreline beyond.

The broad section alongside the shops is a blacktopped parking area, with meters. From here, half a mile from shore, you can watch the 'coaster and listen to its rolling thunder and the joyful shrieks; but the effect is, as a visitor said, "like fishing from a parking lot"; a bit isolated out here and looking across to somewhere else, separated from the place where they're really having fun.

And then a beast starts roaring under our feet. In the water below the fishing wells, two sea lions appear, curving in and out through the pilings, begging for food. . .and then three, four, seven more of them, all laid out on the crossbeams, great furry piles (a bit moth-eaten), sleeping in the late sun slanting in. How do they get up there—climb on when the tide is higher? A little old lady is down on her knees fishing with a drop line in one of the wells, ignoring all their fuss.

This outer end is strictly for fishing: cars are excluded, and there are tables and benches, and a fast-food stand. Fishermen here get surf perch and smelt, and also cabezon, kelpfish and ling cod. The bottom is sandy, but a variety of debris, including 1,092 tires, has been put down to create artificial reefs. Farther back there are two hoists for launching smaller boats, and skiffs for rent.

On the main stem of the pier are several seafood restaurants, some more elegant than others; mostly noisy, crowded, moderately priced and with good food—steamed clams, shrimp, smoked salmon or albacore in a salad, several kinds of fresh fish, and little deep-fried squid (calamares) with curly tentacles, looking like crusty flowers. A surprise: the chowder was Manhattan style, but pink instead of spicy and flaming tomato, and still clam-tasting.

Three curio stores have all the stuff you remember, ashtrays and shot glasses that say *Santa Cruz California*, fantastic shells found far from here, T-shirts and ladybug magnets and fish-shaped plastic combs.

At the fish market you can walk away with a shrimp cocktail or a cup of smoked fish. A four-foot wolf eel was laid out ceremoniously, its blunt head and bulldog, scraggle-toothed jaws fierce and glowering. "Good eating," someone said, as someone usually does about weird-looking creatures.

Commercial fishing began at Santa Cruz in the 1870s with several Genovese fishermen who took their little lateen-sailed boats out in the bay and hauled their nets along the beach...some of their descendants operate local fish markets and seafood houses. Only a few boats bring fish into the pier now—they're moored out in the water, between here and the beach.

The first wharves were built, as usual, to ship out local goods; redwood, lime, tanned leather, paper and potatoes, and then the gunpowder which was manufactured three miles up the San Lorenzo River. The very first, in 1853, was actually a chute from the cliff at the foot of Bay Street, down which bags of potatoes were slid into waiting rowboats: then it was remodeled to carry train-cars of lime which ran down by gravity, and were pulled back up by horsepower.

In 1875, another transformation: this became the Railroad Wharf, with a narrow-gauge railway built on it. The powder works built their own pier in 1863, and the two were connected for a few years by a center section very popular with fishermen.

From the beginning Santa Cruz understood its natural charms, and labored to attract potential tourists. The amusement zone really began more than a century ago, in 1860 when Leibbrandt's Bathhouse, with swimming tank and entertainment hall, was built along the beach.

Early visitors to Santa Cruz arrived by train, and usually stayed several weeks or the whole summer. Southern Pacific ran its first train into town in 1878; by 1887 it was making two round trips daily, with extra excursion trips on weekends.

Participants in the first Save the Redwoods campaign argued that these unique trees also were an important tourist attraction, and in 1902 they persuaded state legislators to create Big Basin State Park, the first state park in California.

By 1904 the beachfront casino stood where it does now, with a 300-cottage Tent City opposite it. All the cottages had electricity, wooden floors and three-foot wooden wainscoting, with multi-striped canvas above, and rented for $3.50-$10 a week.

The two-story casino housed a ballroom, shops, a theater seating 2,500, and a 3,500-seat convention hall; from its roof garden you had a panoramic view of the bay and the Pleasure Pier built out from the casino. There passengers could board the launch *Sinaloa*, first commercial speedboat in these parts, or ride out to the three-masted *Balboa* anchored opposite, to enjoy its seafood grill and the quartet playing dance music.

That first casino burned spectacularly in 1906, and was rebuilt in time for the next season. John Philip Souza, Bryboni's Hungarian Band and other notables played in the Grand Ballroom, the Cocoanut Grove, which was finished off with brass balconies and real silver in the Ladies' Room wallpaper.

The old Railroad Wharf had begun to sag badly, and river silt settling around it was making it too shallow for deep-water vessels; so the town voted to build the present pier, long enough to reach deep water. Its 2,043 pilings of Douglas fir, sent up from Weed, were each seventy feet long and driven twenty feet into the ocean bottom, so the pier could bear the weight of a loaded freight train.

Arrival of the steamer *Roanoke* with a shipload of passengers from San Francisco formed the centerpiece of the pier's dedication on December 5, 1914; but the days of coastal traffic were waning. The last train came off the pier in 1922, and in 1938 the rails were pulled up: the pier was left to the fishermen and the overflow from beach, boardwalk and casino, which continued to thrive.

In the early days no ladies were allowed in the casino saloon, and the bartender there worked fifteen hours a day, getting a few hours of sleep across the street in Tent City. In 1924, the Giant Dipper opened on the Santa Cruz Boardwalk. Now the last wooden 'coaster operating on the West Coast, it's considered one of the ten best in North America—in 1976, it carried its twenty-millionth passenger. The sole survivor; why? Lucky, maybe, that there's no Disneyland close by.

Across the water, above the beach, the yellow-buff casino stands, asymmetrical, horizontal grooves wrapping around one corner. The attached funhouse's arcade, fresh-painted with maroon and green to bring out the details, is a series of narrower arches and then one, two round-headed arches for variation, all of it topped by maroon roofs and crowned by that perfect half-sphere dome. Finishing it off, a flagpole dead center, tall enough but not too tall, and the American flag, the whole broadcasting a hearty and unquestioned self-confidence—a palace dedicated to innocent (if marketable) pleasures, where pleasure is respectable, an institution. Not a relic: a survivor.

Back down the long pier, heading for shore. . .the sun is just setting behind the low hills that rim the town. An old man works his way along the rail, casting, reeling as he walks, fishing all the way back. Beside the beach, along the seawall (twenty feet deep it goes) a kid with a guitar leans against a palm tree watching two others horsing around.

Under the big dome a world of machines, video, pinballs, target practice, bells and pink-and-yellow lights popping. Out along the covered arcade, string bikinis and frozen bananas, the skyride for the big picture and the Dipper rattling and then the roaring plunge and the shriek going up, perfectly predictable.

Far out the water is still blue, dimmed along the horizon by a narrow gray ribbon. On the pier, buildings and cars and people are still edged in sunlight, but the understructure is in shadow; black, solid and graceless—strong enough to carry a freight train we don't need any more. And some of the things we do; summer days, and Saturdays, and holidays. . . .

PILLAR POINT HARBOR PIER

ow, L-shaped Pillar Point Pier sits placid behind its breakwater and surrounded by boats ranging from dinghies to seventy-footpurse seiners tied up along the end, making repairs. Neat, new and pleasant, it's a popular destination for peninsula dwellers who drive over to stroll in the sunshine (if they're lucky), watch the boats moving through the harbor, and do a little fishing, pole or hand-line.

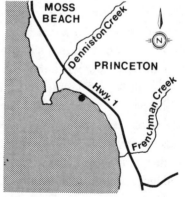

Because of the sandy bottom they can catch several varieties, including flounder, and perch and croaker as well. The sportfishing boats based here—their offices are back of the parking lot—go out for rock cod all year, and ling cod, salmon and albacore in season.

Hazel's Pier, still shown on many maps, is long gone: it was built out where the red building stands, a little upcoast from the pier. Along the shore toward the point, the little community of Princeton-by-the-Sea has boats for sale, and boats in all stages of construction and repair in nearly every open lot. Romeo's Pier, the

113

older pier with the green buildings, belongs to the Romeo Packing Company: it's not public, though the beaches alongside are.

This beach, sheltered by the point and the harbor's north breakwater, is often used to launch catamarans and windsurfers. Since the harbor breakwaters were built in 1959-60, they've caused serious erosion of the coast road beyond the south jetty. Waves from the west come straight in there—in fact, it's a good surfing spot; but the sand is shifting southward, and the jetties keep it from being replenished.

At the upper end of Half Moon Bay, this protected spot behind Pillar Point has been used as an anchorage since earliest times. The Spanish explorer Portola, stopping here with his men, named the place Las Pulgas. They were looking over a rancheria abandoned by the Indians, and soon discovered why: it was hopping with fleas *(pulgas)*. When Europeans settled in this vicinity and began to raise produce, small ships anchored behind the point were loaded by men who waded out with bags of grain on their shoulders. By 1858 a wharf was built out to deep water; and in the 1860s Portuguese whalers set up a whaling station at this spot, and at Moss Beach and Pescadero Point.

The boldest structure conceived for loading goods onto the coastal schooners was Gordon's Chute, located halfway between Pillar Point and Pigeon Point. At Tunitas, on rocks at the foot of a 110-foot-high bluff, Alexander Gordon built a massive superstructure bearing a chute to slide goods from the clifftop to an apron at the bottom which was swung onto the deck of a ship.

But there were problems: ships could load only in the best of weather, since they had to tie up to a reef in the open ocean with no protection; and when the bags of grain or potatoes slid down the long chute, the friction burned holes in them, or they burst when they hit the deck. Gordon's venture went bankrupt, and the sea finished off Gordon's Chute.

Shipping of a sort revived here in Half Moon Bay during the 1920s with the coming of the rum-runners, drawn by the combination of isolated coves, good roads nearby, and a thirsty market not too far away. Among the rum-running "mother ships" was the British steamer *Ardenza*, which sailed from Leith, Scotland, through the Panama Canal to Half Moon Bay with 25,000 cases of Scotch whisky. For seven months in 1924 she stood off this coast in international waters, while contact boats from San Francisco brought out provisions and supplies and took off 18,000 cases of Scotch.

Few traces remain of the whaling ships and coastal schooners which once put in here. Glossy restaurants and antique shops have sprung up among the squash fields along Capistrano Road, and the Pendleton Market has had a facelift. And the big saucer-ears up on the point, part of the Air Force's Space and Missile Test Center, are aimed at swifter craft sailing quite a different ocean.

PACIFICA PIER

Massive Pacifica Pier, newest fishing pier on the coast, stands in water which is anything but pacific. Its tall concrete pilings are designed to keep it above even the biggest storm waves, and on a windy summer afternoon its deck sways faintly as the big green breakers smack through it. The hexagonal pilings angling out from the pier are supplemented at intervals by wider-braced pilings, and two metal expansion plates in the concrete deck allow it to flex in the sea surge.

115

Greer Ferver, the San Diego engineer who designed Pacifica Pier, first hired an oceanography firm to research wave conditions in this area. "They review records of past storms," he said, "and give us design waves—different heights, periods between waves. Then we can determine the magnitude of possible forces on the piles." Ferver's design got its most severe test to date in the winter 1983 storms, when the pier suffered only a couple of broken light standards.

Besides storm waves, piers are constructed to resist earthquakes and support maximum deck loads. "I always tell people—you can't design anything that Mother Nature can't ever top," Ferver said. He's also designed Aliso Pier in Orange County and Ocean Beach Pier, San Diego, and docks and harbor facilities in San Diego, Oregon and Hawaii.

The 1,110-foot pier, finished in 1973, is walled with a broad band of concrete which angles inward above and below the pier deck. The horizontal slits piercing this wall from the outside appear to be in the middle of the wall, but are actually at deck level, allowing water to drain off and the sea air to circulate inside. The pre-cast pilings were set in place by a giant eight-legged device the contractor named Spider, which was mobile but not seaworthy: according to a resident, after the pier was finished Spider tipped over in heavy seas and cracked a couple of the pilings.

The pier ends in a north-pointing L. Fishermen out here were using big poles and squid for bait, catching a few good-sized kingfish and some perch. Pacifica has established itself as a good fishing pier, with a wide variety of fish taken. At the base of the pier, the hexagonal tackle stand and snack shop has a variety of bait, including pile worms, which are found locally, growing under mussels, but can't be taken for sale in California: these are imported from Maine.

Pacifica is the first pier to be built at this spot, on a sandy stretch of wide, flat beach facing the open ocean, with the high hills of the peninsula rising behind. Only a few miles from San Francisco, the area's isolated feeling is enhanced by the dark craggy coastline, Mussel Rock to the north and Mori Point southward, with the heights of Pedro Point and the Montara Mountains beyond. Spray from the thundering surf hangs along the beach, and patches of fog move up the hills toward the ridge.

The blue roofs inland and to the left mark Oceana High School, and on the hill above the freeway, framed by cypresses, is The Castle, a local landmark suggesting a Scottish castle. At various times a medical center, a hideout for bootleggers, and a headquarters for the Coast Guard, it's now a private home.

The little town behind the pier, flat for two blocks back to the freeway, looks to have been here for quite a while; but Pacifica is actually a late-comer among California cities. Partly to prevent the city of San Bruno from coming over the ridge and annexing a strip of the sea, Pacifica incorporated itself in October 1957, when five smaller towns joined together.

Back in 1905, when the Ocean Shore Railway Company began building its way south from San Francisco along the coast toward Santa Cruz, its construction gave birth to the villages of Edgemar, Salada and Brighton Beach, now all part of Pacifica. The railway had reached Pedro Point and the Devil's Slide area when the 1906 earthquake pushed most of the roadbed and much of their equipment into the ocean.

Eventually the rail line reached Half Moon Bay, and then as far as Tunitas, with the opposite end built out from Santa Cruz to Swanton. The Ocean Shore was never finished, and Sunday excursionists going down to Santa Cruz were carried across the twenty-six-mile gap by Stanley Steamers. The railroad carried passengers and freight till 1920, when improved roads, trucking and the automobile put the company out of competition, and withered the villages along the line.

Salada and Brighton Beach eventually joined to become Sharp Park. Pacifica is anchored on Sharp Park State Beach, and just to the south are the Sharp Park Golf Course and a rifle range and archery range, all public. There's also good surfing at several spots.

But fishing is Pacifica's main attraction. Catches here include ling cod, rock cod, all kinds of surf perch, cabezon, and even striped bass. The striped bass is no native: in 1879, 132 small bass brought from New Jersey were released near Martinez, and in 1882 another 300 were released in Suisun Bay. Obviously the climate suited them—they're now found from the Columbia River to the Mexican border.

King and silver salmon are also taken on the pier, according to the owner of Coastside Tackle No. 2, up on the corner of Francisco and Paloma. He showed us a picture of two silver salmon, caught the week before. Over the railing.

FORT BAKER PIER

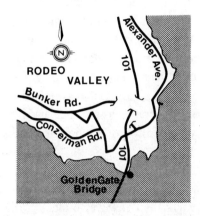

The million-dollar view from Fort Baker Pier is free, and so are the fish—when they're biting. Lying below and inside the north end of the Golden Gate Bridge, the pier is a left-over loading wharf that once served the military installation. Its broad, naked L-shaped platform faces the San Francisco skyline across the bay. A separate lower concrete pier along its west side combines with it to form a U. High overhead on your right, from two great red towers swings the Golden Gate over the water. . . from the pier you hear the intermittent clang of metal from the passage of heavy trucks, or the wind shaking the metal plates of the roadway.

In the throat of the bay on a Sunday afternoon in June, fishermen were wrapped up in hooded and padded windbreakers and knit caps, bracing themselves against the stiff wind—coming not through the Gate, but sweeping down over the headlands. Across the water Alcatraz, the Bay Bridge, downtown skyscrapers and the wooded slopes of the city lay veiled in haze, despite the wind whipping up whitecaps. Streamers of fog reach in from the ocean, and the tops of the thrusting towers are invisible.

But the fishermen, thirty-some city dwellers, Anglo and Oriental, have no time for the view: the smelt have just begun to hit. They're bringing them in two, three, four at a time. . . one man with six hooks on his line reels it in with a smelt flipping on every hook.

Most of the fishermen are using pile worms for bait, cut in little pieces. "They stay on the hook better," one says. "Cost $2.60 for a dozen—expensive. You buy two, three only."

A husband-and-wife team has their gear loaded on a tall cart, back in the center of the pier, and their big white plastic bucket is already full of twitching, splashing fish. They keep running back to it, she in high-heeled boots, crouching to unhook their fish, baiting up again and whipping out the multi-hooked lines with the red plastic float, while less successful fishermen stand quietly and watch.

Near the corner of the pier, sitting on a tie-down once used to secure ships, a man without a pole fishes with a handline wrapped around a spool. Farther on a kid reels in a big smelt, grinning. "One hook, one fish," he says.

Behind on the shore, the neat lawns and red-roofed white buildings of Fort Baker sit quiet and apparently deserted. Both fort and pier are now part of Golden Gate National Recreation Area, created by Congress in 1972. The 38,600-acre park includes twenty-eight miles of shoreline, cliffs and beaches: the Muir Headlands, redwood groves, Fort Mason (where park headquarters are located), and Alcatraz. Golden Gate is a new-style national park, an urban park intended to serve mainly nearby city-dwellers.

Part of Fort Baker is now the non-profit California Marine Mammal Center. Big concrete basins once used to store submarine nets and mines have been converted to pools where rescued seals and porpoises will be treated before being released.

Both fort and pier are dwarfed by Golden Gate Bridge, one of the world's notable engineering achievements. Begun in 1931, its 4,200-foot center span was longer than any ever built. But the most difficult part of the job was building the footing for that south tower: construction conditions here resemble those of the open sea, further complicated by violent currents. The tower rises 1,125 feet from shore, at a spot where the channel is more than 300 feet deep in places, and the fender surrounding it is as big as a football stadium and twice as high. Opening of the bridge in 1937 provided easier access to the north coast, and promptly boosted the population of Marin County.

Located only six miles from the San Andreas Fault, the bridge is designed to sway thirty feet at the top of its twin suspension towers, and its roadway, besides having horizontal expansion joints, can rise and fall as much as sixteen feet with temperature changes.

Completion of the bridge meant an end to the San Francisco-Sausalito ferries, which curved around to eastward and stayed well away from this dangerous spot where the tidal current reaches six knots at maximum ebb. In dense fog on a Saturday evening in 1901, the ferries *Sausalito* and *San Rafael* met almost head-on out in the channel. Before the *San Rafael* sank twenty minutes later, all but three of her 260 passengers were rescued—the only passengers ever lost in sixty-plus years of ferry operations.

Always something happened in the bay...about fifteen boats are anchored now around that big rock next to the bridge, fishing. Sailboats shoot past, heeled over, and the harbor cruise boat loaded with tourists noses into the swells, taking water over the bow sometimes and soaking a few. The overcast thins; the water comes up blue, and the TransAmerica Building and all the city's remembered jigsaw-profile sharpens. Fishing with a view.

Please do not drop your cigarette butts on the floor.
Our cockroaches are getting cancer.
— Sign in cafe, Noyo Harbor

NOYO HARBOR PIERS

Seen from the high trestle bridge spanning the mouth of the Noyo River, Noyo Harbor's jumble of massed boats, trailers, buildings, docks, piers and moving boats form a brilliant contrast to the dark tree-rimmed slopes which hold it like a deep cup. Through its heart the river curves, emptying into the ocean between high bluffs and protecting jetties.

Sportsmen's Dock is closest to the river mouth on the north bank, with boats for

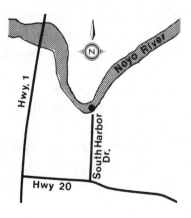

GREAT PIERS *of* CALIFORNIA

rent, a hoist, gas, tackle and a coffee shop. Next over is Custom Canning, where you can have your catch canned when you bring it in, and then a little trailer park, motels, fish markets and waterfront restaurants edged with floating docks.

Commercial boats are moored on up the north bank of the river under the trees, their decks piled with new fishing nets blue or green with gray floats attached, or older nets, rusty brown and edged with ropes of rubber disks cut from tires and strung like leis.

A boatyard, marine engine works and a boat basin with 330 sport boat moorings lie on the south side around the bend, where the river makes a U-turn; and there are cement launching ramps on both sides of the river. Also on the south side, the high pier in front of the little red harbormaster's building gives you some idea of the river's height when it's swollen with winter rains.

When that tsunami (tidal wave) hit Noyo in '64, several waves came in over a four-hour period, the largest two over thirteen feet—powerful enough to damage 100 boats and sink 20 more, including the partyboat *Cavalier*.

Mendocino County's rocky coast is popular with skindivers, who find red abalone still plentiful in this area; but deepsea fishing is the biggest attraction, and salmon is king. Commercial fishing started here in the 1880s, around the time the first sawmill and wharf were being built just upcoast at Fort Bragg in 1885.

The first cargo of lumber out of Fort Bragg was carried by the steam schooner *West Coast*, captained by James Higgins. Believing the new harbor unsafe, Higgins refused to bring his ship in to pick it up until C.R. Johnson, the town's founder, had himself rowed out to the schooner and persuaded Higgins it was safe. Higgins' caution had stood him in good stead: he was then over eighty, having been a shipmaster for more than sixty years. After his initial skepticism, he made several more trips in and out of Fort Bragg without incident.

At that time, wharves were being built along this rocky coast in a dozen "dog-hole" ports—anyplace big enough for a dog to turn around in—to move the lumber being consumed by city-building farther south. Negotiating river mouths and rocky coves was tricky even in good weather; and sometimes, to get back to sea in unfavorable conditions, the sailors rowed the ship's anchor out to sea in the work boat and dropped it. A sailor on board would then pull the ship out with the hand winch. This process was repeated until the boat was clear of the reefs, and out where it could safely take the wind and sail away.

Early fishermen netted silver salmon on the Noyo during the winter, and went out to sea after rock and ling cod and halibut in the summer, being mostly unaware of the big king salmon, though a few were sometimes caught on set lines. A fisherman from the Baltic remembered trolling for salmon there, and in 1898 he

went fishing out of Noyo with a flasher made from a silver tablespoon, and caught two king salmon, the larger thirty-two pounds.

Local fishermen began trolling for the big salmon with dories and skiffs, salting them down for winter use...one day two men fishing from a rowboat in the harbor at Cleone, just north of Fort Bragg, caught forty-eight king salmon, many over fifty pounds and the largest seventy-six pounds.

In 1914 the newly completed railroad enabled local fishermen to pack their catch in ice and ship it out express to San Francisco. Canneries and processing plants were opening along the river. By 1939, the demand for vitamin-rich shark's liver made shark-fishing lucrative—the price for the livers zoomed from 85¢ per pound in '39 to around $12 in 1945—but when Vitamin D was synthesized, the shark liver market vanished. That year also marked the beginning of processing fish netted by the purse seiners: Noyo sole, cod and other fish are now shipped frozen across the United States.

Fort Bragg and Noyo salute the salmon with a big salmon barbeque every summer, with proceeds used to feed fingerlings raised here and released in winter, in hopes of restoring the salmon population to something like its former state. Big communal barbecues with adjustable grates are set up early in the morning, and thousands feast on salmon broiled over chunks of redwood, and salad, bread and corn on the cob.

And then some of them get back to business. Just before sunset a boat heads out of the river mouth already extending its outriggers, elegant silhouette unfolding in a pool of melted-butter light and, arms outspread, pushes on....

EUREKA MUNICIPAL WHARF

L umbering built Eureka, and lumber and fish sustain this city, largest in California north of Sacramento: standing on the wharf in the middle of Eureka's waterfront, the evidence is all around you. Across Humboldt Bay on the North Spit, the smokestacks of Louisiana-Pacific's mill send up plumes of smoke day and night. The streamers can be seen all along the bay, a fine indicator of wind direction as they shift like a great soft white weathervane.

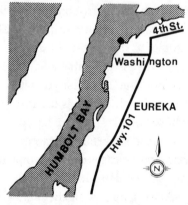

Eureka's Municipal Wharf mixes business with pleasure, as do most waterfront docks. Fishermen along the stem were hauling in good-sized perch, while on the wide T end a man with a fork-lift loaded boxes of just-arrived goods into waiting trucks. The docks are lined with boats, as commercial salmon fishing is closed this

124

week. Salmon is important to the local economy, with more than $13 million worth caught here commercially every year.

For the sportfisherman, the Fish and Game Department says, Eureka has the best catch-per-hour rate of any pier from Oregon to Pismo. And a young couple with a pyramid trap baited with fish heads were catching perch and crabs in it. "Chowder for dinner," said she.

You can also fish from other docks from piers along here, although they're private. Three boys digging and groping in the bright black mud next to a piling pulled out flat, spiky-edged worms more than a foot long—pile worms, prized as bait.

That big island out in the bay, connected to Eureka and the North Spit by two bridges, is Indian Island. Eureka's Fort Humboldt was garrisoned between 1853 and 1865 because of trouble between Indians and settlers, the most violent incident involving the island. In February 1860, the remnants of two or three tribes were encamped there, the warriors being away hunting and fishing, when a group of white settlers massacred the women, children and old people. The returning Indians sought revenge, and months of bitter warfare followed.

The vast expanse of Humboldt Bay, fed by three rivers, is so well-concealed by its two long sandspits that it wasn't discovered until 1806—and then was "lost" again till 1849. Early settler James Ryan drove his ship onto the mud flats in 1850, and exclaimed, "Eureka!"—in Greek, "I have found it!"

Early shipping was hindered but not halted by the dangerous harbor entrance, which could only be taken when conditions were right: one day in November 1881, sixteen ships loaded with lumber crowded around the entrance, waiting to cross the bar. The ocean broke on the sandbar across the entrance, with a depth varying from ten to sixteen feet. "It is often very difficult to get over, and always very rough," a visitor wrote that year.

After crossing the bar, the channel was only a quarter-mile wide for some distance, and three tidal currents in the bay meet at the entrance. Waves up to forty feet high sometimes break over the jetties which now protect the entrance to the harbor.

From 1850 to 1880, twenty-six ships were wrecked on or near the Humboldt Bar, and at least seventy-two people lost. Nevertheless, by 1881 there were twenty-two sawmills producing lumber in Humboldt County, most of it shipped out here, and two steamship lines serving Eureka. That year the largest vessel yet built in California, the 150-foot barkentine *Uncle John*, was launched on Humboldt Bay. The little blue-and-white *Madaket*, used now for harbor cruises, was also built here in 1910, and has operated on the bay ever since.

The harbor cruise is a good way to get some sense of the bay's size and its life.

In the mooring basin north of the pier boats of all sizes tie up, from sailboats to the largest "drag boats," or purse seiners, and alongside you can sometimes see a catch being cleaned by a line of workers at Lasio's Fish Company.

Along the shore the rotted pilings of old piers once serving sawmills and canneries now provide roosts for pelicans and cormorants. Most of the oysters harvested in California come from these tidal flats; south of the wharf you can see a huge cone-shaped pile of shucked shells at the processing plant. The sawmills opposite produce lumber of all sizes, plywood and wood pulp, subject to the economy's building demand—the immense tawny pile alongside is wood chips. Long chutes over the water use compressed air to pump the wood chips directly into a ship's hold.

On the shore of the North Spit lay a small white fishing boat aground and tilted over with half its deck submerged. The week before, as it came into the harbor it was driven onto the rocks of the north jetty. The Coast Guard rescued the two men aboard; tides and currents carried the abandoned boat through the entrance and deposited it here.

As late as the 1950s, local skippers brought back the biggest catch of all. The last whaling station in the United States operated on Humboldt Bay at Field's Landing, three miles south of Eureka. Opened around 1939, during the '40s the industry was part of the war effort: the oil produced glycerine for explosives, and the tenderloin or backstrap section of the whale was edible (though recipes recommend soaking the ruddy meat in vinegar before cooking), and required no ration stamps.

Sperm whales were preferred for the large amount of oil in their heads, but humpbacks and other varieties were also taken. At the plant the whales were hauled up a ramp, butchered on the flensing deck, and their flesh rendered in giant vats. In the first six months of 1943 the station shipped out 250,000 pounds of whale meat for human consumption.

By 1951 residents of Field's Landing were thoroughly fed up with the whale reduction plant. A letter in the *Humboldt Times* signed by fifty-four residents declared that they had done their part for the war effort—"We held our noses till the spring of 1945"—but the stench was no longer tolerable: even the longshoremen working on nearby docks were "losing their dinners to the live fish."

A complaint to the local health department brought the response that a stink never killed anybody. "All we want," the residents' letter concluded plaintively, "is for the station and plant to be operated the same as Eureka fish companies." Shortly afterwards the whaling station was closed and dismantled. Not a whiff of it remains.

TRINIDAD PIER

Trinidad Pier lies alongside Little Head in a peaceful, rock-studded cover sheltered by Trinidad Head, to the right out of the picture. Jailhouse Rock is off the end of the pier.

Trinidad Pier stands in a setting of such stunning natural charm that it could hardly be spoiled—though some have tried. The cove's north arm is the great mass of Trinidad Head, rising 380 feet to a crown thickly grown with clumps of trees and coastal vegetation of lush fog-born green, its dark rocky sides falling sheer to the water. Out in the cove the sportfishing boats and salmon trawlers are moored among smaller knobs of the same rock.

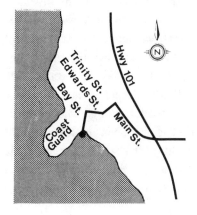

The red-railed pier lies in the lee of Trinidad Head, in water so calm there is no surf on fair days. Alongside towers the smaller dome of Little Head, likewise thatched with shrubbery and trees whose twisting roots squeeze along the stone clefts as though both it and its great cousin were bent on imitating the picturesque extravagance of a Japanese landscape painter. A row of bright-painted dinghies fringes the floating dock alongside the pier, the whole a visual feast.

Add to this, fishing here is excellent. At the sink on the lower level of the pier, two fishermen were cleaning their day's limit of silver salmon, taken four or five miles out at fifteen feet in twenty-fathom water. Up on the deck a boy cleaned a fifty-three-pound halibut he'd just brought in.

Owned now by Bob Hallmark but still open for public use, Trinidad Pier was constructed for sportfishing in the late '40s, built with contributions from the Arcata Lumberjacks' Association. The buildings on its outer end, the domain of Hallmark Fisheries, once housed a crab-processing plant.

The Yuroks who first inhabited the cove called their village Tsurai or Cho-ri, the jumping-off place. On Trinity Sunday in 1775 the Spanish explorer Heceta landed here, and accordingly named the spot Trinidad.

A gold strike in 1849 on the Trinity River twelve miles away made Trinidad the first settlement in the Humboldt Bay region, this being the nearest anchorage to the gold diggings, and in a year the town had 3,000 residents. That long rock off the end of the pier shaped like a chaise lounge is Jail Rock, where rowdy inhabitants were marooned overnight to cool down. The local gold rush died, and two years later Trinidad's population was nil.

In the 1870s logging revived the town somewhat, with a sawmill built at the foot of the bluff, and the first wharf constructed alongside Trinidad Head, where the water was thirty feet deep at low tide; the steamer *Mary D. Hume* called here regularly on her way from San Francisco to Crescent City. They say you can still see the cable attachments in the rock, used to load the lumber. A heavy cable attached to a buoy was picked up by the ship and fastened to its mast, and the lumber was hauled in swing loads along the cable attached to a trolley.

On the seaward face of the Head, a lighthouse, Trinidad Head Light Station, was built in 1871 and stands 196 feet above the sea. In December 1914, the lighthouse keeper witnessed a southwester which produced unusually heavy seas for a week—though sheltered from the prevailing winds moving downcoast, Trinidad lies open to storms which come from the south. In his log he recorded that at 3:00 P.M. on December 31 the seas increased, and a number of waves washed over Pilot Rock, which is the tallest rock you see in the cove, half a mile out and 103 feet high.

An hour and a half later he saw an enormous sea rise 200 yards out. It hit the bluff with a jolt like an earthquake, shaking the tower and stopping the revolving light; barreling up the face of the cliff and landing as solid water at the level of the lighthouse 196 feet above mean high water, nearly engulfing it.

Whaling came fairly late to Trinidad, in 1920 when a whaling station began operating just where the pier is now, its first whale being a fifty-two-ton humpback, a female. Whale oil sold for seventy-five cents a gallon then, and the oil from eight of them could fill a railroad tank car. These whalers used hundred-foot steamers with swivel cannon mounted in the bow which shot a 150-pound harpoon attached to a six-inch manila line 2,000 feet long. Whale oil was used to make soap and cosmetics, its meat and bones for fertilizer. The station took 620 whales before it shut down in 1926 and moved out to sea, where it could operate more cheaply.

Today you can watch the whales passing on their winter migrations. Some people insist that they come inshore to scrape off their barnacles on the rocks.

A restaurant, the Seascape, sits at the foot of the pier, overlooking the harbor, and behind Little Head is Trinidad's unique boat hoist, a 250-foot railroad slanting into the sea. Boats are hoisted onto a small railroad car and run by pulleys down the track and into the water. The first year the sea surge kept dislocating the rails, and skindivers went down to anchor the seaward end: the standard gauge tracks come from old logging camps, and have to be replaced often. Only damage to the pier itself has been during winter storms when a big log comes in or a boat gets loose and smashes into it.

Trinidad today is a town of 300, with tackle and gift shops, restaurants and motels, and a neat, little complex with market and post office beside Highway 1.

"This used to be a nice quaint little place," a fisherman said, watching the big halibut being cleaned. "Now it's all commercial. People on vacation catch some salmon, have a good time—then they decide they want to make some money out of it, and they start catching salmon every day just to sell. See, they can't just relax and have fun...some people have to push, make a buck even on vacation."

It could be worse. In 1967 a corporation wanted to buy Little Head, blast it off to a height of twelve feet above the pier, and build a restaurant and cocktail lounge on it. But Little Head is still there.

CRESCENT CITY
CITIZENS DOCK

Passengers prepare to board the steamer *Del Norte* at the Crescent City Wharf around 1908. The *Del Norte* also has a deck load of lumber and other cargo. Whale Island, left, is now part of the harbor breakwater.

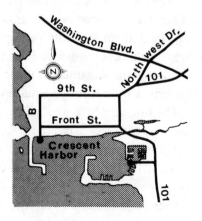

Citizens Dock lies in the center of Crescent City Harbor, walled around with tall jetties of gray rock like fortifications holding back the sea. On a calm, overcast morning the harbor waters reflect gray sky and boats moored alongside, and it's hard to visualize the stormy seas which regularly batter this coast...in fact, from here you barely see the ocean.

But winter storms and high tides crash over the broad causeway of the south jetty which connects the shore with Whale Island. From Whale Island a breakwater right-angles 1,200 feet across the harbor, ending opposite the pier—a 95-foot Coast Guard cutter is berthed alongside it, available for rescue work.

Beyond it but invisible from the pier, the 4,700-foot arm of the north jetty, anchored on Battery Point, bends around to form a broad, protected entering channel for the commercial and sportfishing boats based here. Both the outer jetty and the pier were severely damaged in a tsunami (tidal wave) in 1964, which sank twenty-one fishing boats and submerged downtown Crescent City under twenty feet of water.

To strengthen the breakwater it was then repaired with 1,630 tetrapods of cast concrete, each weighing twenty-five tons—you can see one of the tetrapods alongside the highway from the south, just where it turns to enter the town. Shaped rather like child's jack, tetrapds have few plane surfaces and don't slide over one another, making them more durable. Instead they're locked together more tightly by the wave action, even as they let the water flow through.

Named for its crescent of beach, the town lies on a coastal plain ringed by the low wooded hills typical of the north coast, the dark sawtooth contours of their fir-covered slopes often blurred by the fog drifting over the crests, drawn up from the sea.

Memories of that night in March 1964 are vivid here, though nothing remains of the damage but several broken-off pilings beside the pier. California's northernmost pier, Citizens Dock, had been built entirely by donations of local materials and labor. The rebuilt pier measures 900 feet, with a 100-foot L end where commercial fishermen unload their catches of salmon, crab, shrimp, albacore and bottom fish—in 1978 a total catch of 18,356,500 pounds came into this harbor. The *Lucky Star* from Seattle, tied up alongside the dock, belied her name: her engine room charred and half gone, she was being used for storage.

With slips for 306 commercial boats north of the pier, and moorings for 305 smaller craft, the harbor also gets a large number of boats in transit; 245 during May 1979 alone. Salmon fishing is a major attraction—in the ocean during the summer, in local rivers October-December. Inside the south jetty there's a cement ramp for launching trailered boats, with tourist attractions nearby; The Underseas Gardens, a walk-through aquarium, and a seafood restaurant and a tackle shop.

The first pier here was built on Whale Island in 1855 by a whaling company which established its station on the ten-acre rock to render the whales they caught along the coast. Whalers on their way to Alaska, and other ships, too, anchored in the lee of the island, which could be either side, depending on which direction the storm came in.

In the late 1800s coastal shipping increased as newly-established communities grew, and the violent and unpredictable sea caused many a shipwreck. The worst disaster here was the wreck of the steamer *Brother Jonathan*, which went down in a summer storm in 1865 with 232 aboard, of whom only 11 reached shore alive. Treasure-hunting divers still search for the gold some believe the *Jonathan* was carrying.

Caught in a northwest gale on its way to Portland from San Francisco, the *Jonathan* had already passed Crescent City when, shortly past noon, the captain ordered the quartermaster to put about and head for this harbor. Seas were running "mountain high": it was clear in the vicinity of the ship, but "foggy and smoky" inshore. Somewhere around Point St. George, seven miles north of Crescent City, the ship struck a rock, foundered and began to break up in the heavy seas.

Of the six lifeboats launched, most immediately swamped or capsized. Only one lifeboat reached the beach at Crescent City, about five o'clock that afternoon, to tell the story. The sinking of the *Jonathan* took about forty-five minutes, according to survivors, and those trapped on board reacted in various ways. James Nisbet, editor of the *San Francisco Bulletin*, sat on the deck and wrote out his will and a farewell note to a friend—the pencil-written will was found in a purse in his breast pocket when his body washed ashore two days later. Ironically, California state courts refused to honor this will, because it lacked witnesses.

On earlier voyages the *Jonathan* was known to have carried gold from the Idaho mines, as much as $500,000 at a time. Fired by rumors of an Indian who had recovered a chest full of five-dollar gold pieces, and a shipment of one million dollars in Canadian gold aboard, the lure of sunken treasure has kept interest in the lost ship *Jonathan* evergreen. Periodically divers set out to search for it.

The problems are many: at least eleven other sunken ships lie in these waters; divers must work in 100 feet of water, and the passage of time has thoroughly disguised the wreckage.

"The trouble is, what with currents and whatnot, there's only about two weeks in August that you can dive on it," the man operating the boat launch told us. "And every winter the wreck shifts again in the storms, and you can't find it again for five years."

On Battery Point, just beyond the base of the outer breakwater, stands a lighthouse which is now a maritime museum, and among its relics is a bell from the *Brother Jonathan*. You have to wait for low tide to walk out to the lighthouse, just as the lighthouse keepers and their families did in the past.

In 1860 the first shoreline wharf was built here, only to be destroyed by severe storms the next year. But its successor stood for more than sixty years, handling everything from lumber, butter and passengers to gold dust and the U.S. mail. The pier served as shipping point for the Hobbs, Wall Lumber Company, which in 1903 ran a spur from its sawmill out onto the wharf. When steamships reached Crescent City in heavy fog, they were guided to the pier by short blasts of the sawmill whistle, answering the whistle from the ships.

When the company shut down its mills in 1939, the pier fell to pieces. Citizens of the town, seeing themselves in the heart of the fishing and redwood lumbering industries with no docking facilities, had tried five times over thirty-two years to get the government to finance a dock; with no success. In 1949 somebody suggested, "Let's build it ourselves." And they did; the town of 3,000 providing all the lumber, tools, equipment, pilings, rockfill and labor. It was dedicated on March 18, 1950, in a howling rainstorm which drove everybody indoors for the ceremony, followed by a feast of local Dungeness crab.

Harbor, dock and town faced their severest test fourteen years later, on March 28, 1964, when an earthquake in Alaska created a tsunami which hit the waterfront shortly after midnight.

The first wave covered Front Street with water, and brought in some logs. After an interval the second wave hit, with less force, and then the third; but as the third wave receded, said an eyewitness, "The entire harbor was emptied like a huge basin, and boats were laid over on their sides. There was so little water that a person could have walked out to the jetty without getting wet."

As the fourth wave rolled over the jetty, cresting at 20.78 feet, it picked up lumber, pieces of deck and any loose debris, and drove them into whatever lay in its path. It stacked up the dock planking like a washboard and knocked pilings sideways. Parked cars and trucks were swept up, rolled over and smashed through storefronts. Huge logs washed down the rivers in earlier storms and lying on Del Norte beaches punched through walls and lodged inside buildings.

Twenty-nine city blocks were inundated: broken power lines arced and exploded: five huge fuel-storage tanks blew up and burned, and fires also destroyed two oil plants and three downtown businesses. One man was trapped in a closet in Daly's Department Store as the water rose, pushing his face against the ceiling with only inches to spare before it receded. Damage totalled $16 million. When the four-hour siege ended and the waters receded, eleven people were dead.

"Actually, they were used to tidal waves here," said Helen Williams, curator of the Del Norte County Museum. "Whenever they had one, people used to say, 'Let's go downtown and see what damage it did.' But never anything like this."

Crescent City has had at least seven smaller tsunamis since '64, none of them causing much damage. Since their rate of speed can be estimated, the townspeople can be warned in time; and Crescent City now has a warning system, a siren with a distinctive wail. They blow it once a month, on a Thursday.

Bibliography

Newspapers Consulted

The Argonaut (Venice)
Easy Reader (Hermosa Beach)
Del Norte Triplicate
Five Cities Times-Press-Recorder
Humboldt Standard
Humboldt Times
Huntington Beach News
Long Beach Independent
Los Angeles Free Press
Los Angeles Herald Examiner
Los Angeles Times
Monterey Peninsula Herald
New York Times
Ocean Beach News

Orange Coast Daily Pilot
Port Hueneme Press-Courier
Reader (Ocean Beach)
San Clemente Independent
San Diego Evening Tribune
San Diego Union
San Luis Obispo Telegram-Tribune
Santa Ana Register
Santa Barbara News Press
Santa Cruz Sentinel
Santa Monica Outlook
South Bay Daily Breeze
Ventura Signal

Magazines

Architectural Design, Jan. 1971
Architectural Review, May 1969; Dec. 1970
Grizzly Bear, Dec. 1924; May, 1946
Los Angeles & Redondo, Vol. 15, #1, Feb. 1957
Los Angeles County Museum of Natural
    History Quarterly, Spring 1967
Los Angeles Magazine, March, 1965
Newsweek, Aug. 12, 1946; Aug. 19, 1946

San Diego Magazine, Dec., 1974; Aug., 1976
Saturday Evening Post, Aug. 12, 1939
Southwest Building Contractor, Jan. 16, 1920
Sunset, Jan. 7, 1908
Time, Aug. 19, 1946
Touring Topics, Sept., 1925; Aug., 1927; Dec.,
    1916; Oct., 1932
Westways (19 references)

Agencies Consulted

California Department of Fish & Game
Wildlife Conservation Board
City & County Departments of Public Works,
    Parks & Beaches, Parks & Recreation
Various Harbor Districts

Orange County Environmental Management
    Agency
U.S. Army Corps of Engineers
Numerous local historical societies

Books

American Guide Series, Federal Writers Project of Work Progress Administration *California, A Guide to the Golden State* 1939.
—— *Monterey Peninsula* 1941.
—— *Santa Barbara* 1941.
Avila Beach Centennial Program Pamphlet in San Luis Obispo Public Library, 1976.
Banks, Homer *The Story of San Clemente   The Spanish Village* Self-published, 1930.
Best, Gerald M. *Ships & Narrow Gauge Rails: The Story of the Pacific Coast Company* Howell-North, 1964.
Brown, Giles G. *Ships That Sail No More* Kentucky University Press, 1966.
California Department of Transportation *Final Construction Report, Ventura Pier* Sacramento, May 3, 1950.
Caughey, John & LaRee *California Heritage* Ward Ritchie Press, 1962.
Caughey, John & LaRee *Los Angeles, Biography of a City* University of California Press, 1976.
Crump, Spencer *Ride the Big Red Cars* Crest Publications, 1962.
Donaldson, Steve *Santa Ana and Newport Railway* Booklet 395, The Western Railroader, 1975?
Dumke, Glenn *The Boom of the Eighties in Southern California* Huntington Library Publications, 1944.
Filosa II, Gary *The Surfers' Almanac* E.P. Dutton, 1977.
Friis, Leo *Orange County Through Four Centuries* Pioneer Press, 1965.
Gleason, Joe D. *The Islands and Ports of California* Devin-Adair Co., 1958.
Gordon, Ron *Complete Guide to Monterey Peninsula* Typescript in Monterey Public Library; 1975.
Hicks, John & Regina *Cannery Row, a Pictorial History* 1972.
Higgins, Delbert O. *Huntington Beach Piers* Typescript in Huntington Beach Public Library, n.d.
Hill, Lawrence L. *La Reina, Los Angeles in Three Centuries* Security Trust & Savings Bank, 1929.
Hopkins, Harry *History of San Diego: Pueblo Lands and Water* 1929.
Hutchinson, W.H. "The Fight for Hueneme Wharf" *Ventura County Historical Society Quarterly*, Vol. XVII, No. 4 (1939), 19-24.
Ingersoll, Luther A. *A Century History of Santa Monica Bay Cities* 1908.
Johnson, Ken *Fun, Frustration & Fulfillment: An historical study of the City of Redondo Beach*, Bound typescript, Redondo Beach, 1965.
Koch, Margaret *Santa Cruz County: Parade of the Past* Valley Publishers, 1973.
Lamb, Frank W. & Gertrude *San Simeon   A Brief History* Sultana Press, 1971.
Lee, Ellen *Newport Bay, A Pioneer History* Newport Beach Historical Society, 1973.
Lenihan, J.M.A. *The Marine Environment, Vol. 5* Academic Press, 1977.
Lewis, Oscar *Fabulous San Simeon* California Historical Society, 1958.
Locale Monterey Savings & Loan, Spring, 1975
Lydon, Sandy & Carolyn Swift *Soquel Landing to Capitola-by-the-Sea* California History Center, 1978.
McCallister, Linda C. *The Waterfront of Manhattan Beach* Manhattan Beach Historical Society, n.d.
McWilliams, Carey *Southern California Country* Duell, Sloan & Pearce, 1946.
Meyer, Samuel A. *Fifty Golden Years: The Story of Newport Beach* Newport Harbor Publishers, 1957.
Myers, William A. & Ira Swett *Trolleys to the Sea* Interurbans, 1976.
Nadeau, Remi *Los Angeles, from Mission to Modern City* Longmans, Green, 1960.
Oceanside Union Title Insurance & Trust Co., 1958.
Reid, Ed & Ovid Demaris *The Green Felt Jungle* Trident Press, 1963.
Reinstedt, Randall *Where Have All the Sardines Gone?* Ghost Town Publications, 1978.
Report of a Structural Study of Stearns Wharf Martin & Northart, Inc. n.d.
Rhein, Fern *Early History of Hermosa Beach* Bound typescript in Hermosa Beach Public Library, 1933.
Robinson, W.W. *The Malibu* Ward Ritchie Press.
Sheridan, Sol *History of Ventura County, California* S.J. Clarke, 1926.
Sherman, H.L. *A History of Newport Beach* Times-Mirror, 1931.
Stanton, Jeffrey *Venice, California, 1904-1930* ARS Publications, 1979.

Vose, Frances *Huntington Beach Since the Turn of the Century, with emphasis on Beach and Pier Area*
    Typescript in Huntington Beach Public Library, n.d.

Walker, Franklin D. *A Literary History of Southern California* University of California Press, 1950.

Water Resources Developed by the U.S. Army Corps of Engineers in California Dept. of the Army, Jan.
    1979.

Welton, Blythe *From Fishcarts to Fiestas—The Story of San Clemente* Self-published, n.d.

Willoughby, Malcom F. *Rum War at Sea* U.S. Govt. Printing Office, 1964.

Wilmington (Pamphlet for 50th Anniversary) Wilmington Savings & Loan, n.d.

Wright, Bank *Surfing California* Manana, 1973.